Enforcing Prophetic Decrees
Volume II

Prayer Watch for
Community Transformation

*Archbishop Nicholas
Duncan-Williams*

2

Also by Archbishop Nicholas Duncan-Williams

Enforcing Prophetic Decrees Vol. I

Prayer Moves God

Powers Behind the Scenes

Divine Timing

When Mothers Pray

The Price of Greatness

The Supernatural Power of a Praying Man

Praying Through the Promises of God

Destined to Make an Impact

Binding the Strong Man

All available at Amazon.com

Enforcing Prophetic Decrees Volume II

Prayer Watch for Community Transformation

Archbishop Nicholas Duncan-Williams

Prayer Summit Publishing
www.prayersummitinternational.org

6

Enforcing Prophetic Decrees Volume II
Copyright ©2016 by Archbishop Nicholas Duncan-Williams

Printed in the United States of America
Prayer Summit Publishing

ISBN: 978-0692770344

All scriptural quotations are from King James Version of the Bible unless stated otherwise.

www.prayersummitinternational.org

Dear Friend,

Blessings upon you! I am excited that you have taken this step in learning more about Prophetic Decrees and the Prayer Watches. I believe that in this End-Time, it is important for us intercessors to pray strategically and with knowledge. As we embark on this journey, may your strength be renewed like the new morning. May you sit in the counsel of the Lord and execute the judgment written to stand before kings and may the Lord give you nations. May He stir up the wells inside of you and increase your firepower and your desire to pray and intercede for your family, city, church, pastor, and nation. May He make you an Intercessor, a priest after the order of Melchizidek. This is your year to be blessed. May your heart be found pure and may kings be your friends. Let doors open and favor overtake you. May every wickedness of the enemy be broken at the dawning of a new day. It is a new season! Behold, let the wells within you spring forth and produce new streams of increase, blessing and greatness in the days to come. You are blessed in the mighty name of Jesus!

-Archbishop N. Duncan-Williams

8

Contents

Introduction

In 2006, I published a book entitled Enforcing Prophetic Decrees volume one, which brought much transformation to people's lives, churches, and communities. My focus in Volume 1 was to introduce the public to prophetic decrees and how to pray with them.

In recent times, my heart has been burdened to write a second volume of the book. In this second volume of Enforcing Prophetic Decrees, my desire is to impart to you the importance of praying through the Prayer Watches and enforcing the decrees for each of those Watches.

In order to enforce the release of the end-time harvest and see Revival come to individuals, churches, cities, and nations, we must be willing to stand in the gap and pray as we take our rightful position as Intercessors. We must overturn by intercessory prayer the plans of the enemy and superimpose the plans of God.

"I will overturn, overturn, overturn, it: and it shall be no more, until he come whose right it is; and I will give it him." (Ezekiel 21:27)

Intercession will precede the coming of the Lord. Revelation 19:7-8 tells us He will return when the Church has prepared herself:

"Let us rejoice and exult and give him the glory, for the marriage of the Lamb has come, and his Bride has made herself ready; it was granted her to clothe herself with fine linen, bright and pure"— for the fine linen is the righteous deeds of the saints."

The fine linen, bright and pure, is the key to our readiness in the Lord. Fine linen is the nature of the creation or garment; bright and pure is the expression of our nature or garment. This means that once we have received salvation, we are now the redeemed of the Lord. But, it is by the righteous acts that we become the regenerated of the Lord – a new creation:

"That ye put off concerning the former conversation the old man, which is corrupt according to the deceitful lusts; And be renewed in the spirit of your mind; And that ye put on the new man, which after God is created in righteousness and true holiness." (Ephesians 4:22-24)

We must make ourselves ready by prayer. It is through the Word of God that we renew our minds and put away the former things to establish the new things:

"And be not conformed to this world: but be ye transformed by the renewing of your mind, that ye may prove what is that good, and acceptable, and perfect, will of God." (Romans 12:2)

We must seek the Lord consistently and regularly in order to be ready when He comes:

"And now, little children, abide in him; that, when he shall appear, we may have confidence, and not be ashamed before him at his coming." (1 John 2:28)

The word "abide" in the above verse is the Greek term *"menō"*, which is generally translated as: "to abide", "to remain", "to stand fast", "to wait", "to hold your position". Abide means to have constant communication with the Lord. He will reveal Himself and His Will through our prophetic intercession. It is through prophetic intercession we are led by the power of the Holy Spirit to pray the will and purposes of God. We do this, under the power of His Word and the inspiration of the Holy Spirit through decrees and declarations.

This edition of Enforcing Prophetic Decrees will focus on the deployment of Intercessors, praying through the Prayer Watches, deploying the five-fold ministry giftings and enforcing the Revival of the Lord for our time and our generation.

Chapter One

Declarations and Decrees

Declarations

The word "*declare*" comes from the Hebrew term "*achvah*", meaning "to make known" or "to set forth an accounting."   Making declarations is an apostolic mandate of the Church to set forth or make known the blessings of God for a person, a family, a church, a nation, etc.

When you as a believer pronounce through a declaration in prayer, you are enforcing the blessing, which the Spirit has already revealed:

"That which we have seen and heard declare we unto you, that ye also may have fellowship with us: and truly our fellowship is with the Father, and with his Son Jesus Christ. And these things write we unto you, that your joy may be full. This then is the message which we have heard of him, and declare unto you, that God is light, and in him is no darkness at all." (1 John 1:3-5)

Prophetic declarations typically denote the blessings of the Lord and involve the enforcement of answered prayer. As seen in 1 John 1:3-5, the Apostles were declaring to the church the message and sure testimony of their eyewitness account of Jesus Christ. A declaration speaks forth and establishes the blessings and promises of God.

Throughout the Gospels, Jesus Christ used the word declare repeatedly to announce the message of the Kingdom of God. He teaches the disciples that when the Holy Spirit comes, He will announce and reveal Christ by declaration:

"However when he, the Spirit of truth, has come, he will guide you into all truth, for he will not speak from himself; but whatever he hears, he will speak. He will declare to you things that are coming. He will glorify me, for he will take from what is mine, and will declare it to you. All things whatever the Father has are mine; therefore I said that he takes of mine, and will declare it to you." (John 16:13-15)

This prophetic declaration was confirmed when the Holy Spirit came on the Day of Pentecost. Scriptures say:

"And in the day of the Pentecost being fulfilled, they were all with one accord at the same place, and there came suddenly out of the heaven a sound as of a bearing violent breath, and it filled all the house where they were sitting, and there appeared to them divided tongues, as it were of fire; it sat also upon each one of them, and they were all filled with the Holy Spirit, and began to speak with other tongues, according as the Spirit was giving them to declare." (Acts 2:1-4)

The Holy Spirit gave them *utterance* or *the ability to declare* as He gives us today when we declare that which we have seen and heard in times of prayer. That is how we use declarations correctly.

Decrees

Decrees, on the other hand, are enforcing the written judgments of the Lord under the inspiration of the Holy Spirit:

"Thou shalt also decree a thing, and it shall be established unto thee: and the light shall shine upon thy ways." (Job 22:28)

A decree is not the same as a declaration. A declaration can speak forth the blessing and reveal the secret things of God. Pronouncing a declaration alone can overturn the plans of the enemy.

But there are judgments in the law of God that must be suspended or superimposed and cannot be overturned. In that situation, a new judgment – a higher law – must be <u>decreed</u> for the Word to be established. The secret to our ability to decree a thing is found in the preceding scriptures:

*"If thou return to the Almighty, thou shalt be built up, thou shalt put away iniquity far from thy tabernacles.... For then shalt thou have thy delight in the Almighty, and shalt lift up thy face unto God. **Thou shalt make thy prayer unto him, and he shall hear thee, <u>and thou shalt pay thy vows</u>**." (Job 22:23, 26-27)*

Now we see there are some prerequisites that must be met before our decrees can be established. Firstly, we must put away iniquity. That means we have to be ready to repent and be willing to have daily fellowship with the Lord. Secondly, we must lift up our eyes to the Lord and pray to Him. Lastly, the Word says we must pay our vows to Him; we cannot be lawless and expect to enforce the laws of God.

So you see, we must hear from the Spirit and make some counter-decrees to overrule the decrees of the enemy. In the Book of Esther, Haman was able to get the king to make a decree that could not be overruled except by a counter-decree:

"If it please the king, let it be written that they may be destroyed: and I will pay ten thousand talents of silver to the hands of those that have the charge of the business, to bring it into the king's treasuries. And the king took his ring from his hand, and gave it unto Haman the son of Hammedatha the Agagite, the Jews' enemy. And the king said unto Haman, The silver is given to thee, the people also, to do with them as it seemeth good to thee." (Esther 3:9-11)

This was the judgment written against the Jews by their enemy Haman. Once the king's ring sealed this decree there was no way to overturn it by mere words (declarations). Even the king could not repeal the written law. He had to write a new law that could be superimposed over the first written law.

Even though Haman had been hung on his own gallows, his property given to Esther and his ring to Mordecai, the wicked decree to annihilate the Jews could not be overturned without a counter-decree. Esther appealed to the king to reverse the judgment written by writing a new law:

"...And said, If it please the king, and if I have favour in his sight, and the thing seem right before the king, and I be pleasing in his eyes, let it be written to reverse the letters devised by Haman the son of Hammedatha the Agagite, which he wrote to destroy the Jews which are in all the king's provinces." (Esther 8:5)

The king favored Esther. The first law was written in his name and sealed with his ring. This second law would also have to follow the same pattern so that it carried the necessary weight to nullify the *preceding* judgment by releasing a *proceeding* judgment:

"Write ye also for the Jews, as it liketh you, in the king's name, and seal it with the king's ring: for the writing which is written in the king's name, and sealed with the king's ring, may no man reverse." (Esther 8:7-8)

Here the king clearly tells Esther that the judgment or decree of the king is final. No one can overturn the written judgment. The Word is powerful my friend. The enemy is always trying to get you to break the commands of God so that he can execute the judgment written against you. This is why it is important for us to pray in accordance to the words in Colossians chapter 2:

"Blotting out the handwriting of ordinances that was against us, which was contrary to us, and took it out of the way, nailing it to his cross;" (Col. 2:14)

The final judgment of the king read:

"And he wrote in the king Ahasuerus' name, and sealed it with the king's ring, and sent letters by posts on horseback, and riders on mules, camels, and young dromedaries: Wherein the king granted the Jews which were in every city to gather themselves together, and to stand for their life, to destroy, to slay and to cause to perish, all the power of the people and province that would assault them, both little ones and women, and to take the spoil of them for a prey," (Esther 8:10-11)

Here we see that the deliverance of the Jews was not automatic. They would need to use the new law to defend themselves against the old law. The people of the provinces would have executed them under the old law, so the new law had to be enforced by the Jews over their enemy in response to the old law. The warfare was still necessary. The new law gave them a new defensive and offensive weapon to defend themselves and to gain the upper hand over their enemies.

The Dominion Mandate Decree

As I set out in more detail in my book "Prayer Moves God," when Adam ceded the dominion of the earth to Satan, we all came under the law of sin and death. Every person must die as a result of sin. God did not repeal the law of sin and death. He sent Jesus to enact a higher law:

"Therefore there is now no condemnation for those who are in Christ Jesus. For the law of the Spirit of life in Christ Jesus has set you free from the law of sin and of death." (Romans 8:1-2)

It took a higher law to destroy the law of sin and death. The higher law is the Spirit of life in Christ Jesus. He is the Superior Sacrifice and His Name is Higher than any other name. His

Kingdom is higher than all the kingdoms of this world, which is why He told us to pray, "Thy Kingdom Come." We must superimpose His Kingdom over the kingdoms of this world. We cannot destroy Satan's kingdom through declarations alone. We must decree a higher law. The book of Esther gives us an example of the warfare that we must fight to deal with the iniquities that continue to resist us and keep us from living victoriously.

This is why we need the ministry of the Intercessor or "The Watchman". Throughout this volume of Enforcing Prophetic Decrees, we will use the term "Watchman" and Intercessors interchangeably. The term "Watchman" or "Watchmen" to describe both the male and the female Intercessor as the Biblical term "Watchman" is gender neutral. Prayer is not for men or women only. All of mankind must lift their voice in prayer generation after generation. This is our Dominion Mandate and how we take authority over the enemy. Beloved, there is a battle already set in motion against us, and we must stand for our life, using the higher decrees of the Lord to defend and take back our territory that was stolen by Satan. We do this through intercession. It is intercession that will precede Revival, the release of five-fold ministry giftings and the promise of the Lord's return. We must raise Intercessors in order to break the resistance, engage in spiritual warfare and enforce the victory of the Kingdom of God.

Prayer Points

- We plead the Blood of Jesus against witchcraft orchestrations and demonic setups deployed to keep us from executing the judgment written over the enemy. Let any decree that disenfranchises or diminishes the righteous receive a counter-decree from the Lord in the name of Jesus.

- Reveal to us the counter decrees to overturn, overrule and override the decrees of satanic powers of darkness in our time, in our nation, in our community, in our family, in our church, etc. so that we can have total victory in the name of Jesus.

- We release the lightening and thunders of God against the witchcraft and marine kingdoms, the forest and the animal kingdom and any workers of iniquity who are using the weapon of satanic manipulation to avert, destroy or delay the promise of God in our life in the name of Jesus.

- We deactivate satanic activations that went into effect at the spoken word over our life. We deploy a counter-declaration to confront and overturn the declarations of the wicked, of false prophets, any contrary voice or spirit of the error of this Age that is preventing the true Word of God from coming to pass over our life, our nation, our family, our church, etc. in the name of Jesus.

- We blind satanic monitors and destroy witchcraft gadgets monitoring our progress, movements and making sure we are denied, delayed or subverted in our course.

- We decree Divine Judgments against demonic command centers assigned to watch over, monitor and enforce curses and attacks against The Righteous and the seed of The Righteous.

- We interrupt any satanic carrier of satanic pregnancies, conceptions and agendas and we terminate and abort their assignment and arrest the carriers of the assignment. We unseat them now in the name of Jesus.

- We interrupt satanic vehicles deployed to kill, to steal and destroy the righteous. Let the vehicle be destroyed and every trusted weapon of the enemy be exposed and destroyed in the name of Jesus.

Confession

Lord I want to be a weapon in your arsenal to pray for the Revival in my family, my church and my nation. Help me to increase my faith, increase my prayer stamina and increase my spiritual giftings so that I can be an effective Intercessor. I will bring my flesh under subjection to the Spirit so that I can be used by you for this next move of God in the Earth. I will do my part to be faithful, committed and obedient to pray daily, consistently and without fail for the assignment you have given me in Jesus name. Amen.

Chapter Two

What is the Role of the Intercessor?

Many of the children of God are called to be prophetic Watchmen or *Intercessors* to release the end-time harvest. But, how do you know if you are called? What is the responsibility of a Watchman or an Intercessor? What are the Prayer Watches? Why should we pray and how often should prayer be made? What is the significance of the time? We will be working through all these questions in this volume of Enforcing Prophetic Decrees.

Let's start first with the role of a Watchman or Intercessor.

The Role of a Watchman or Intercessor

God deployed watchmen over the nation of Israel.

There are three different Hebrew words for the term "*Watchman*" in the Word that has to do with their specific assignment and how to execute that assignment in prayer:
1. Shamar
2. Tsaphah
3. Natsar

"Shamar" means to hedge about (as with thorns), to guard, to protect, to attend to, to be circumspect, to take heed of, to look narrowly, to observe to preserve, to regard, to reserve or save, to lie in wait, to be a watchman. Adam's role in the Garden of Eden was to be a Shamar. He was to guard and protect his territory. (Genesis 2:15, NLT)

"Tsaphah" means to lean forward, to peer into the distance, to observe, to await, to behold, to espy, to wait for, to keep the watch. The activity of the Prophet Habakkuk – the posture he took in prayer – was to Tsaphah, which means that he tarried before the Lord to wait until he heard what to do. (Habakkuk 2:1)

Finally, *"Natsar"* means to guard (in a good sense or a bad one), to conceal, to besiege, to keep, to observe, to preserve, to be a watcher. This is the role of the watcher on the watchtower who is to block the advancement of the enemy on a stronghold. (Ezekiel 33:3-7)

The general role and responsibility of an Intercessor is laid out in scripture in the following verses from the Prophet Isaiah:
"Therefore are my loins filled with pain: pangs have taken hold upon me, as the pangs of a

woman that travaileth: I was bowed down at the hearing of it; I was dismayed at the seeing of it." (Isaiah 21:3)

Here the prophet is describing a *"massa"* of the Lord. The Hebrew term *"massa"* denotes a burden of the Lord that He assigns to the individual to pray about – especially as it relates to nations. Isaiah, Jeremiah and Ezekiel used this term to give prophetic instructions to the watchmen concerning the nation of Israel.

In the book of Isaiah, we note that the prophet bows down and begins to travail in prayer:

"My heart panted, fearfulness affrighted me: the night of my pleasure hath he turned into fear unto me. Prepare the table, watch in the watchtower, eat, drink: arise, ye princes, and anoint the shield." (Isaiah 21:4-5)

He prepares himself for the battle and enters into spiritual warfare. He is prepared to give up his sleep in order to stand watch – abide – as he awaits the instructions of the Lord:

*"For thus hath the Lord said unto me, Go, set a watchman, let him declare what he seeth."
(Isaiah 21:6)*

A Watchman or Intercessor is sent ("Go"), given an assignment ("set a watchman"), and told to declare what he or she sees. The ministry of a prophetic Intercessor can be to a family, a business, a church, a community, a nation or even global. The requirement is that you must be sent, you must be assigned and you must say (declare) what you see.

The Bible records that God's purpose in sending Jesus was for Him to serve as an Intercessor:

*"And He saw that there was no man, and wondered that there was no intercessor: therefore His arm brought salvation unto Him, and His righteousness, it sustained Him."
(Isaiah 59:16)*

Jesus stands before God and between Him and sinful man, just as the Old Testament priests did:

"For there is one God, and one mediator (Intercessor) between God and men, the man Christ Jesus." (I Timothy 2:5)

"...It is Christ that died, yea rather, that is risen again, who is even at the right hand of God, who also maketh intercession for us." (Romans 8:34)

"Wherefore He is able also to save them to the uttermost that come unto God by Him, seeing He ever liveth to make intercession for them." (Hebrews 7:25)

When we accept the assignment to pray and stand in the gap for individuals, for churches, for nations, etc., we move from just merely watching in prayer – we are now elevated to the position of Intercessor. As Intercessors, we take on the role of Spiritual Watchmen. Our role as Intercessors is to reveal the mind of God and the ordinances of Heaven. As Intercessors, God will assign us and speak to us what to pray and what to decree and declare. The Prophet Habakkuk said:

"I will stand upon my watch, and set me upon the tower, and will watch to see what he will say unto me, and what I shall answer when I am reproved." (Hab. 2:1)

He says He will watch to see what the Lord will speak and then he will speak. That is the posture we must take in prayer if we are going to speak the mind of God for people, situations, nations, etc., we must be willing to declare whatever we hear God saying:

"For thus hath the Lord said unto me, Go, set a watchman, let him declare what he seeth." (Isaiah 21:6)

When you are assigned as an Intercessor, the Lord will send you, assign you and require you to sound the alarm by speaking forth His decrees and declarations.

The ministry of the Intercessor is ongoing and consistent. The success of an Intercessor requires consistent, regular and persistent prayers:

"Now when Daniel knew that the writing was signed, he went into his house; and his windows being open in his chamber toward Jerusalem, he kneeled upon his knees three times a day, and prayed, and gave thanks before his God, as he did aforetime." (Daniel 6:10)

Daniel was successful because he studied the Word and knew what needed to be executed in prayer, he prayed regularly and consistently. He did not become discouraged when he didn't see the answer to his prayer immediately. In fact, he prayed until his prayers got Heaven's attention and broke the spiritual resistance:

"Then said he unto me, Fear not, Daniel: for from the first day that thou didst set thine heart to understand, and to chasten thyself before thy God, thy words were heard, and I am come for thy words." (Daniel 10:12)

Here we see that the angel came for the words of Daniel. It was his consistent, fervent prayer that produced the necessary spiritual firepower to bring Heaven into the affairs of men. Our assignment to pray as Intercessors is serious to God and He wants us to take it very serious. He gives us these instructions:

"But if the watchman sees the sword coming and does not blow the trumpet and the people are not warned, and a sword comes and takes a person from them, he is taken away in his iniquity; but his blood I will require from the watchman's hand." (Ezekiel 33:6)

So the Lord has a requirement of the Intercessor when He speaks a word of warning for the Intercessor to sound the alarm and to act as a protector for those who are in the path of destruction. We are responsible for one another.

"Now as for you, son of man, I have appointed you a watchman for the house of Israel; so you will hear a message from My mouth and give them warning from Me. When I say to the wicked, 'O wicked man, you will surely die,' and you do not speak to warn the wicked from his way, that wicked man shall die in his iniquity, but his blood I will require from your hand. But if you on your part warn a wicked man to turn from his way and he does not turn from his way, he will die in his iniquity, but you have delivered your life. " (Ezekiel 33:7-9)

God requires the Intercessor He has set on His assignment to be faithful and committed to that assignment. As He instructed the Prophet Ezekiel, so He still instructs the Church today. We are to pray for one another.

"Confess your faults one to another, and pray one for another, that ye may be healed. The

effectual fervent prayer of a righteous man availeth much.

Brethren, if any of you do err from the truth, and one convert him; Let him know, that he which converteth the sinner from the error of his way shall save a soul from death, and shall hide a multitude of sins." (James 5:16, 19-20)

Let the End-Time Intercessor and the Five-Fold Ministry Arise

The greatest hindrance to the church today is spiritual blindness. The enemy has succeeded in putting the Intercessors to sleep. The enemy has succeeded in putting the five-fold ministry to sleep. The Bible warns us in Psalms chapter 13 that to be caught sleeping or blinded by the enemy can lead to death. Satan wants us to remain blind and silent so that we will not be able to uncover his schemes and we will fall into his snares and traps, taking others with us.

"How long shall I take counsel in my soul, Having sorrow in my heart all the day? How long will my enemy be exalted over me? Consider and answer me, O LORD my God; **Enlighten my eyes, or I will sleep the sleep of**

death, And my enemy will say, "I have overcome him," And my adversaries will rejoice when I am shaken." (Psalms 13:2-4)

Jesus told us to *"watch and pray"* so that we may be found worthy to escape the devices and the snares of the adversary:

"Watch ye therefore, and pray always, that ye may be accounted worthy to escape all these things that shall come to pass, and to stand before the Son of man." (Luke 21:36)

Jesus' last battle with Satan, the death of the Cross, was preceded by an intense time of prayer in the Garden of Gethsemane. He taught us a lesson and a warning about what will happen if we do not remain watchful and pray during times of crisis:

They went to a place called Gethsemane, and Jesus said to his disciples, "Sit here while I pray." He took Peter, James and John along with him, and he began to be deeply distressed and troubled. "My soul is overwhelmed with sorrow to the point of death," he said to them. "Stay here and keep watch." (Mark 14:32-34)

This shows us that in times of prayer there are levels we can enter with the Lord. The Lord needed to enter into travailing prayers. He didn't take all the disciples. He took the ones He had spent the most time with. He told the others to wait for Him to return. However, He told Peter, James and John to "stay here and keep watch." He wanted them to abide in Him. To watch with Him, to enter the realm of intercession and to take on His burden. In Mark 14:35-36, He asks the Father to let the "cup pass from Him." He is distressed and wants to be backed in prayer. He returns to find them sleeping and rebukes them:

"Then he returned to his disciples and found them sleeping. "Simon," he said to Peter, "are you asleep? Couldn't you keep watch for one hour? Watch and pray so that you will not fall into temptation. The spirit is willing, but the flesh is weak." (Mark 14:37-38)

He says to Peter if you don't watch and pray – you will fall into temptation. The spirit is willing but the flesh is weak. We bring the flesh under subjection in prayer.

If we are not willing to watch and pray, we disqualify ourselves and will be found ashamed at the return of the Lord:

"When he came back, he again found them sleeping, because their eyes were heavy. They did not know what to say to him." (Mark 14:40) He shows us that if we don't watch and pray and we permit the flesh to master the spirit, we will give place to the devil and be caught unaware when He returns. We will permit the blinding veil of Satan to cause us to lack illumination and sleep the sleep of death:

"Consider and hear me, O Lord my God: lighten mine eyes, lest I sleep the sleep of death." (Psalm 13:3)

Prayer Points

- We decree a Divine reversal by the Supreme Sacrifice of the Blood of Jesus of every demonic verdict, demonic predictions and demonic prophecies contending with the true promise of God over our life, destiny, our spouses, our children, the church, leadership and our nation in the name of Jesus.

- We override and overturn all impending satanic predictions designed to subvert, destroy, manipulate, contend, or oppose the prophetic word over our lives and enforce what is written concerning us in the volume of the books in the name of Jesus.

- We overrule from the throne room perspective and by the Superior Sacrifice of the Blood of Jesus any satanic agenda, verdict, assignment and impending dangers in the Heavens, on the earth beneath and rising from the waters of the earth.

- By Divine Authority we decree Divine Judgments against all demons that ride on the air, on the winds and on the sea.

- We interrupt and rebuke strange winds designed to bring sudden disaster or to blow us away from our Divine Appointment and keep us from fulfilling our Divine Destiny in the name of Jesus.

- By Divine Authority we reverse satanic handwritings and verdicts against The Righteous and the seed of The Righteous in Jesus name. We superimpose and enforce the Will of God and the judgments of Elohim over The Righteous and the seed of The Righteous in Jesus name.

I will arise from my place of slumber to take my rightful place in the throne room of Elohim. I will not be found sleeping when I should be alert, aware and awake in order to hear what the Spirit is saying to the Church. I will do everything I can so that I do not grieve the Holy Spirit. I will be sensitive to His Voice and His command so I can be effective in prayer and bring community transformation in the name of Jesus.

Chapter Three

The Discipline of Prayer

Prayer – A Spiritual Discipline

Prayer is a spiritual discipline. In fact, God wants us to pray at all times and He uses our prayers as a weapon to enforce His purposes for the earth. The Bible says you are God's weapon:

"Thou art my battle axe and weapons of war: for with thee will I break in pieces the nations, and with thee will I destroy kingdoms; And with thee will I break in pieces the horse and his rider; and with thee will I break in pieces the chariot and his rider." Jeremiah 51:20-21

It is our voice lifted in prayer that permits God to execute His battle strategy. God will not intervene in the affairs of men until someone prays. He commands us to pray all kinds of prayers for one another:

"Praying always with all prayer and supplication in the Spirit, and watching thereunto with all perseverance and supplication for all saints." (Ephesians 6:18)

In the Old Testament, God separated the priesthood from the congregation, however ALL of God's people were commanded to watch. The Bible says in 2 Chronicles:

"But let none come into the house of the Lord, save the priests, and they that minister of the Levites; they shall go in, for they are holy: but all the people shall keep the watch of the Lord." (2 Chronicles 23:6)

In the New Testament, however, all believers are admonished to pray for one another and to be ambassadors for Christ as we are called to the Royal Priesthood. The Bible says:

"Ye also, as lively stones, are built up a spiritual house, an holy priesthood, to offer up spiritual sacrifices, acceptable to God by Jesus Christ." (I Peter 2:5)

"Now then we are ambassadors for Christ, as though God did beseech you by us: we pray you in Christ's stead, be ye reconciled to God." (2 Cor. 5:20)

God is using you and I to bring others to Christ. When we pray, we are standing in the gap for our family, our church, our cities, our nations and anyone God wants to reach. Our assignment is to use the vehicle of prayer to reconcile others to Christ. Our daily prayers are a daily sacrifice for daily triumph.

"I beseech you therefore, brethren, by the mercies of God, that ye present your bodies a living sacrifice, holy, acceptable unto God, which is your reasonable service. And be not conformed to this world: but be ye transformed by the renewing of your mind, that ye may prove what is that good, and acceptable, and perfect, will of God." (Romans 12:1-2)

We present our bodies as a living sacrifice through our daily prayer life. When we set aside time to pray and wait for the Lord, He will reveal to us the secrets of the Kingdom and His Will for us, our families, our churches, our cities, the Church and our nation. When we pray daily and consistently, it permits us to abide in His presence and God will trust us with Revelation. This is what happened when Peter received the keys to the Kingdom.

Praying for Illumination and Revelation

In the book of Luke chapter 9, Peter gets a revelation from the Father of who Christ is and the Lord releases the keys to the kingdom.

"And it came to pass, as he was alone praying, his disciples were with him: and he asked them, saying, Whom say the people that I am? They answering said, John the Baptist; but some say, Elias; and others say, that one of the old prophets is risen again. He said unto them, But whom say ye that I am? Peter answering said, The Christ of God." (Luke 9:18-20)

Jesus was praying for the disciples in Luke 9:18 after a great miracle had been performed. The miracle of the fish and loaves was a benchmark in the life of the disciples because, for the first time, they were not just observers of the Kingdom but had directly participated in the miracle of the fish and loaves. When you become an Intercessor, God is using you to participate in the establishment of the Kingdom of God over the kingdoms of this world.

Jesus whilst praying asked the Father to give his disciples illumination. In order for you to hear from Heaven, you must be awake in the spirit and receive illumination. When Peter responded and identified correctly the revelation of who Christ is, Jesus said He would use that revelation to build His Church. The prayers of Jesus gave Peter access to the throne room to receive revelation from the Father about who Jesus is. After Peter received the Revelation, Jesus gave him the keys of the Kingdom of Heaven to bind and to loose.

The keys to bind and loose are very important in intercession. You will need keys of revelation to pray effective prayers.

Keys signify revelation and it enables you to know what to bind and loose in prayer. To have dominion on the Earth, you must have revelation of the ordinances of Heaven. You have to know what is bound in Heaven and what is loosed in Heaven so that you can walk in dominion:

Knowest thou the ordinances of heaven? Canst thou set the dominion thereof in the earth. (Job 38:32)

Revelation enables you to know what Heaven has already determined concerning issues and matters of the Earth and this revelation gives you audacity to walk in dominion on the Earth. This is the power of an Intercessor.

"But ye are a chosen generation, a royal priesthood, an holy nation, a peculiar people;

that ye should shew forth the praises of him who hath called you out of darkness into his marvellous light." (I Peter 2:9)

As believers, we are a kingdom of priests who have the responsibility to restore others to the family of God and prepare them for His coming:

"And from Jesus Christ, who is the faithful witness, and the first begotten of the dead, and the prince of the kings of the earth. Unto him that loved us, and washed us from our sins in his own blood, And hath made us kings and priests unto God and his Father; to him be glory and dominion for ever and ever. Amen." (Revelation 1:5-6)

In order to be an effective Intercessor, you will need wisdom and revelation. You must pray daily and often to build a relationship with the Holy Spirit that develops your ear to hear Him and that opens the eyes of your understanding so that you may know "what is the hope of His calling." This is what is needed today to receive the rich rewards of our inheritance in Christ Jesus:

"Wherefore I also, after I heard of your faith in the Lord Jesus, and love unto all the saints, Cease not to give thanks for you, making mention of you in my prayers; That the God of our Lord Jesus Christ, the Father of glory, may give unto you the spirit of wisdom and revelation in the knowledge of him: The eyes of your understanding being enlightened; that ye may know what is the hope of his calling, and what the riches of the glory of his inheritance in the saints." (Ephesians 1:15-18)

Prayer Points

- Command every satanic altar that is a power base for any satanic decree against your life and destiny to be demolished. Any power base that is being used to fight your prayer life or diminish your ability to focus in prayer – let it be destroyed in the name of Jesus.

- Command every satanic covenant that has been established to give the enemy a legal right to any dimension of your life to be reversed and destroyed. Let the voice of the Blood overrule the voice of any satanic covenant that prevents you from accessing the realm of the Spirit in Jesus name.

- Command any satanic calendar operating in conjunction with any satanic altar and covenant to be destroyed by the fire of God.

- Command every distraction and objection coming from the dark kingdom that prevents you from being sensitive to the Holy Spirit to receive the Fire of God be destroyed now in the name of Jesus.

- Command the effects and consequences of all charms, spells, enchantments, divination, sorcery and every witchcraft activity against your prayer life and the Grace to pray travailing prayers to be aborted and destroyed by the blood of Jesus Christ and the fire of God.

- Command any person with or without a body that is being used to distract you and keep you from a life of prayer to be arrested and for their assignment to be terminated and destroyed.

- Command any demonic cycle, persistent situation or perpetual circumstance that has become a hindrance and a blockage to you praying regularly; command it to be overturned by the power of the Holy Spirit in the name of Jesus.

- Command focus, concentration and tenacity in prayer to be your portion in the name of Jesus.

Confession

I will be an Intercessor and exercise my role as a Watchman. I will be sent, assigned and able to sound the alarm because I am disciplined, faithful and obedient to the call of God on my life in the name of Jesus. Thank you Lord for choosing me for the great work to bring in the end-time Harvest. Amen.

Chapter Four

Setting Aside Time to Pray

Setting Aside Time to Pray

To be effective we must set aside time to seek the Lord. The Word of God tells us we must seek the Lord while He may be found:

"Seek the LORD while He may be found; Call upon Him while He is near." (Isaiah 55:6)

God is waiting for us. As much as prayer is a time to wait upon the Lord, He is truly waiting to instruct, guide and provide us with wisdom and revelation to destroy the works of darkness and enforce the Kingdom of God.

"Call to me and I will answer you and tell you great and unsearchable things you do not know." (Jeremiah 33:3)

In order to be disciplined in our prayers, we should follow the instructions laid out in the Word of God. He tells us that there are benefits to praying during the various watches of the day:

"Evening, and morning, and at noon, will I pray, and cry aloud: and he shall hear my voice." (Psalm 55:17)

God has set times when He will meet us when we are dedicated to pray. He will come looking for us to fellowship and speak with us. We know that God looked for Adam in the coolness of day.

David prayed three times a day:

"Evening, and morning, and at noon, will I pray, and cry aloud: and he shall hear my voice." (Psalm 55:17)

"Now when Daniel knew that the writing was signed, he went into his house; and his windows being open in his chamber toward Jerusalem, he kneeled upon his knees three times a day, and prayed, and gave thanks before his God, as he did aforetime." (Daniel 6:10)

Jesus often withdrew to the desert to pray and His habit was to pray:

"However, he continued his habit of retiring to deserted places and praying." Luke 5:16

Jesus admonished the disciples to develop a habit of consistent prayer and to be tenacious and persistent in their prayers. He also talked to them about times of prayer.

"And he said unto them, Which of you shall have a friend, and shall go unto him at midnight, and say unto him, Friend, lend me three loaves; For a friend of mine in his journey is come to me, and I have nothing to set before him? And he from within shall answer and say, Trouble me not: the door is now shut, and my children are with me in bed; I cannot rise and give thee. I say unto you, Though he will not rise and give him, because he is his friend, yet because of his importunity he will rise and give him as many as he needeth. And I say unto you, Ask, and it shall be given you; seek, and ye shall find; knock, and it shall be opened unto you. For every one that asketh receiveth; and he that seeketh findeth; and to him that knocketh it shall be opened." (Luke 11:5-10)

Jesus reveals that we must ask, seek and knock in prayer. This is travailing prayer. This kind of prayer comes by consistently praying until what we have is not only received, not only found, but is opened unto us.

The book of James in the New Testament gives us an example by describing the fervent prayers of Elias:

"Confess your faults one to another, and pray one for another, that ye may be healed. The effectual fervent prayer of a righteous man availeth much. Elias was a man subject to like passions as we are, and he prayed earnestly that it might not rain: and it rained not on the earth by the space of three years and six months. And he prayed again, and the heaven gave rain, and the earth brought forth her fruit." (James 5:16-18)

God has times and seasons during our life when He is looking to fellowship with us so that He can speak to us and build our relationship with Him. God is looking to meet us during set times of prayer:

"Give ear to my words, O Lord, consider my meditation. Hearken unto the voice of my cry, my King, and my God: for unto thee will I pray. My voice shalt thou hear in the morning, O Lord; in the morning will I direct my prayer unto thee, and will look up." (Psalms 5:1-3)

We must set aside time to pray and be dedicated and committed to meet God during those times and seasons of prayer. Pray regularly. Pray often. Pray without ceasing. Pray with purpose. Pray with prayer:

"Elias was a man of like passions to us, and he prayed with prayer that it should not rain; and it did not rain upon the earth three years and six months." (James 5:17a)

If we will be obedient to meet Him in prayer, He will help us to pray by Revelation for the Church, the nations, the communities, the families, etc. to which we are assigned so that we can truly see and experience Revival Fires. Prayer is not just by knowledge, but prayer is by revelation. The most effective prayers are the prayers we pray by revelation.

Prayer Points

- By Divine Authority I enter the realm of the Spirit and access the secret place around the throne of God.

  I confront and destroy the root of laziness and lethargy that prevents and opposes me planning and preparing to hear from God at set times during the day or night in the name of Jesus.

- By persistent prayer I prepare myself for greater capacity. I call for the Fire of God to destroy the weapons of distraction and complacency that that the enemy uses to prevent my progress and to destroy my purpose in the name of Jesus.

- By the Blood of Jesus, I destroy the weapons of fear and intimidation that the enemy uses to cause me to not walk in faith and plan for the impossible to become possible in the name of Jesus.

- I destroy the trusted weapons the enemy uses to make me miss my Kairos moment and any time-sensitive blessing, open door, relationship or revelation that is needed to establish my God-given purpose in the earth in the name of Jesus.

- From the Throne Room perspective I exercise my Divine Right as a believer and follower of Christ to access the realm of the supernatural and pull down the invisible things of God into the visible realm of the Earth that will be a blessing to my family, my community, my church and my nation in the name of Jesus.

- I decree by Divine Authority I will not miss my God-given opportunities and God-ordained relationships because of poor planning and lack of capacity to receive the abundant supply God wants to bless my family, my community, my church and my nation.

- I deploy the Word written in Psalm 35:27 that says God takes pleasure in the prosperity of His servant and the Word written in Zechariah 1:17 that says, "My cities through prosperity shall yet be spread abroad," and I decree that it is the Lord's pleasure to prosper me, my family, my community, my church and my nation in the name of Jesus.

Confession

God I commit to be faithful to meet you at an appointed time during the day or night to enforce your agenda in the earth. Help me find the Prayer Watch you have called me to and give me the Grace I need to be obedient to keep the time appointed. Teach me, guide me, lead me, speak to me and help me as I seek you and find out your revelatory plans in the name of Jesus. Amen.

Chapter Five

Destroying Satanic Veils

Destroying Satanic Veils

We must pray to destroy the satanic veils covering those who are called to be Intercessors in this generation. It is by prayer that we communicate with God to bring the heavenly decrees, revelatory purposes and written judgments of the Kingdom of God into the Earth realm and override the power of the Kingdom of Satan.

Adam was the first Watchman or Intercessor and when he ceded the Dominion Mandate to Satan, he compromised his position and gave Satan a foothold in the affairs of the Earth. Until Adam's lease expires, Satan still rules over the affairs of men and that is the main reason why prayer is a daily necessity for daily triumph. We cannot cease praying. It is our job to pray, it is Satan's job to resist our prayers. Satan puts up a resistance when we pray, but we must remain vigilant. The Word of God says:

For we wrestle not against flesh and blood, but against principalities, against powers, against the rulers of the darkness of this world, against spiritual wickedness in high places. (Ephesians 6:12)

As long as Satan has the lease that Adam ceded to him, prayer is the necessary tool to enforce God's original intent and bring the Kingdom of God on the scene in the affairs of men. It is in prayer that we exercise not only our dominion over the Earth but we take authority in the Heavens and over the interference of the enemy who is the prince of the power of the air – the blinding veil that blocks our heavens.

"And he will destroy in this mountain the face of the covering cast over all people, and the vail that is spread over all nations." (Isaiah 25:7)

This veil blocks us from receiving revelation from the realm of Heaven to keep us in the dark so that we never know what is happening behind the scenes. The veil keeps you ignorant so that you blame God for what is going on and you fail to recognize the schemes of the enemy that is operating to wreak havoc and destruction. Once the veil is lifted by illumination through prayer you are empowered to overrule the works of the enemy.

"Lest Satan should get an advantage of us: for we are not ignorant of his devices." (2 Corinthians 2:11)

The main purpose for the veil is to keep us blinded in the dark, ignorant, desensitized and eventually to discredit the Word of God to the believer so that we stop believing God's Word and we blame God for everything bad that happens to us. Because God sees all things and He is all knowing, we expect that He should prevent bad things from happening to us. But, as I expounded in my book "Prayer Moves God" God gave man dominion over the earth and the rules of engagement require that we pray, intercede and use the Word of God to overrule, override and overturn the works of darkness. By discrediting the Word of God, Satan gets us to deny our faith and lose our hope in God's ability to help us. That is what Satan did to Adam and Eve in the Garden. He discredited the Word of God – which is our source and our weapon to destroy the veil and to keep him from operating behind the scenes. We use the Word to expose the works of darkness.

We must overrule the works of darkness and destroy the blinding veil by using the Word of God to pray and bring God on the scene.

Prayer Points

- Pray that any man or woman, any person with or without a body that is using spells, incantations, witchcraft, sorcery, human or animal sacrifices or any of the tools of evil to transact through money, tokens, witchcraft or any other mischief that has become a veil– let them be overturned and let their works backfire in the Name of Jesus

- Pray that anyone that is attempting to hijack the destiny and future of the Intercessors of this generation – let them be located, uncovered, and arrested and let their sacrifices, projections, spells, incantations and all their works be overturned, overruled and rendered null and void by the Supreme Sacrifice of the Blood of Jesus in the Name of Jesus.

- Let them fall and never rise again in power. Let their veil be destroyed by Fire. Let them fall into any pit or snare they have dug for the righteous and the seed of the righteous.

- Let the projections of the wicked be overruled and overturned by the judgment written. Let them be broken in pieces and let the Intercessors of this generation be strengthened in the name of Jesus

- Superimpose God's original agenda for nations over any other agenda of the enemy. Overthrow the agendas of evil men and spirits and let the will of God be done over your nation in the name of Jesus.

- Pray that any mischief devised to hurt your nation be overturned and backfire on those behind it

- Arrest spiritual armed robbers that attempt to hijack national resources or attempt to destroy the people in strategic positions to help the nation and attempt to blind the citizens of the nation so that there is unrest and destruction – let them be arrested now in the name of Jesus

- Rebuke all forms of spiritual assassinations and assassins attempting to destroy the righteous and the seed of the righteous so that the nation loses its direction and focus and becomes obsolete and insignificant. Let them be revealed, exposed, uncovered and destroyed in the Name of Jesus.

- Release the fire of God and the illumination of understanding that destroys satanic veils and the hidden agenda of the enemy to set the nation back and prevent the advancement of the nation and its people in the name of Jesus.

Confession

Today, by Divine Authority, I overrule, overturn and override the agenda of Satan to keep me blind, to blind my nation, my community, my church, my family and any work my hands have been assigned to do – let the Hand of God deliver me and bring illumination that destroys the veil and breaks the resistance so that I can prevail over all the works of the enemy in Jesus Name I pray. Amen.

Chapter Six

How Revival Comes

Releasing the Intercessors by Prayer

The enemy will not release those held captive unless he is bound and his diabolical opposition against the Kingdom of God is destroyed. It is through prayer that the prison doors are opened. We must pray and deploy Angelic assistance to break satanic resistance. We must pray without ceasing to enforce their unconditional release.

The Church prayed for Peter and an Angel was released.

Peter therefore was kept in prison: but prayer was made without ceasing of the church unto God for him. (Acts 12:5)

The enemy will not just release captives because we confess scriptures. We must pray without ceasing to deploy angelic assistance.

And, behold, the angel of the Lord came upon him, and a light shined in the prison: and he smote Peter on the side, and raised him up, saying, Arise up quickly. And his chains fell off from his hands. And the angel said unto him, Gird thyself, and bind on thy sandals. And so he did. And he saith unto him, Cast thy garment about thee, and follow me. (Acts 12:7-8)

If we will pray with force, God will do miraculous things that exceed our imagination.

Now unto Him that is able to do exceeding abundantly above all that we ask or think, according to the power that worketh in us. (Ephesians 3:20)

Paul and Silas prayed at midnight – a key time for intercession – and their prayers were answered in a way no one could have imagined:

And at midnight Paul and Silas prayed, and sang praises unto God: and the prisoners heard them. And suddenly there was a great earthquake, so that the foundations of the prison were shaken: and immediately all the doors were opened, and every one's bands were loosed. (Acts 16:25-26)

We must pray to release the Intercessors of this generation. The Intercessors of our nations will need to be prayed for so that they can take their position. This is why now is the time to gather together and accept the Call to Watch and Pray. This is why I am asking you to become a member of The Network of Global Prayer Intercessors and join a Prayer Watch Team to pray for your nation, your city, your church, your family, and to bring Revival to this generation. {See information on becoming an Intercessor in the Epilogue of this book.}

When we release Intercessors, we will see Revival and tremendous growth come to the Church. In Acts chapter 3, Peter heals a man who sits at a gate called "Beautiful" and 5000 men are added to the church. Scripture says:

"Now Peter and John went up together into the temple at the hour of prayer, being the ninth hour. And a certain man lame from his mother's womb was carried, whom they laid daily at the gate of the temple which is called Beautiful, to ask alms of them that entered into the temple; Who seeing Peter and John about to go into the temple asked an alms. And Peter, fastening his eyes upon him with John, said, look on us. And he gave heed unto them, expecting to receive something of them. Then Peter said, Silver and

gold have I none; but such as I have give I thee: In the name of Jesus Christ of Nazareth rise up and walk. And he took him by the right hand, and lifted him up: and immediately his feet and ankle- bones received strength. And he leaping up stood, and walked, and entered with them into the temple, walking, and leaping, and praising God. And all the people saw him walking and praising God: And they knew that it was he which sat for alms at the Beautiful gate of the temple: and they were filled with wonder and amazement at that which had happened unto him. And as the lame man which was healed held Peter and John, all the people ran together unto them in the porch that is called Solomon's, greatly wondering..." (Acts 3:1-11)

Uncovering the Strongman

There are issues hidden in the shadows of our personal lives, our families, our churches, and our nations and we are often prevented from seeing it.

Now, you cannot deal with it unless you see what you're dealing with. So, you have to remove the covering. When you remove the covering, then you can see what was hidden.

You must uncover anything hidden in the shadows responsible for your pain, responsible for your depression, responsible for your setback. It must be uncovered for you to spiritually see.

The responsibility of an Intercessor is to uncover those things hidden in the shadows - the Strongman that hides in the shadows.

In the account of the man healed at the Beautiful Gate that we read above, Peter and James uncover the Strongman who sits at the Gate of Israel. The ninth hour of the Prayer Watch is 3pm. In further chapters, you will learn the various watches of the day and the prayers to pray during those watches. The ninth hour (3pm) is a time to make declarations to change the course of a nation. Here we see Peter and John approach the temple in the presence of all Israel gathered and, as was the custom, they brought the lame man to the Gate to beg.

There are a few things to consider. Firstly, note that Peter and James are at a *strategic gate*; this gate is the entrance to the temple where the people come to seek the God of Israel and to discuss the affairs of the nation.

Secondly, this is the entrance to Solomon's Porch – known as the "Women's Court" or the place where the women came to pray. This gate is a strategic opening and they have come at a strategic hour.

Every nation has a gate and the enemy wants to make a proclamation and decree evil, but when we take our position as Intercessors we can issue counter decrees to overturn the decree of the enemy.

The man at the Beautiful Gate is physically lame, but spiritually he represents a statement about the Nation of Israel that is being proclaimed at the Gate. The statement is that there is no Healer in Israel. Peter does not merely see the man as lame, but he sees the opportunity to bring the Healer to the Nation of Israel:

"And Peter, fastening his eyes upon him with John, said, Look on us." (Acts 3:4)

Peter goes behind the scenes and looks through the shadows to deal with the Strongman at the gate.

In Peter's declaration for the man to rise up and walk in the name of Jesus, he is declaring The Healer has arrived in the Nation and when he reaches his hand out to the man, it is not the hand of Peter, but the Hand of God that brings an immediate solution to the Nation of Israel:

"And he took him by the right hand, and lifted him up: and immediately his feet and ankle bones received strength." (Acts 3:7)

When the man enters Solomon's Porch, he has entered the place where the women are praying and the Bible says the people came out wondering what had happened at the Beautiful Gate.

"Repent ye therefore, and be converted, that your sins may be blotted out, when the times of refreshing shall come from the presence of the Lord." (Acts 3:19)

Peter's declaration is not about the man. He is making a declaration to the nation to repent and be revived. If we are going to experience the healing that comes from national revival, we are going to have to repent as a nation.

"And as they spake unto the people, the priests, and the captain of the temple, and the Sadducees, came upon them, Being grieved that they taught the people, and preached through Jesus the resurrection from the dead. And they laid hands on them, and put them in hold unto the next day: for it was now eventide." (Acts 4:1-3)

Now, the healing took place at the ninth hour (3pm). But, by the time Peter is done preaching the Gospel and admonishing the people to repent, a full Watch (3 hours) has passed. It is now evening time. An Intercessor must hold their position. An Intercessor may face opposition, accusation, misrepresentation and even reproach. But, hold your position! Stay persistent in prayer and go behind the scenes to arrest the strongman and reveal the ordinances of heaven.

The effect of the prayers, the Miracle of healing and the Word that Peter preached that day had supernatural consequences. Scripture says:

"Howbeit many of them which heard the word believed; and the number of the men was about five thousand." (Acts 4:4)

Peter ministered at a strategic gate (Beautiful) from a certain hour of prayer (the ninth hour) for a specific period of time (until eventide) and the Church grew by 5000 men. Beloved, if we are going to see a move of God and experience Revival, we will have to dedicate ourselves to pray and to be strategic in our prayers.

Pray To Avert Judgement

When a nation is dry and there is enmity between the fathers and the children, God has made a decree in Malachi 4:5-6 which says:

"Behold, I will send you Elijah the prophet before the coming of the great and dreadful day of the Lord: And he shall turn the heart of the fathers to the children, and the heart of the children to their fathers, lest I come and smite the earth with a curse."

Elijah the prophet was a Prophetic Intercessor over the Nation of Israel. By his word, the heavens refused to give rain. When he travailed again in prayer, it began to rain. It will take travailing prayers to break the spiritual drought and release the rain of Revival.

When a nation enters apostasy and no more regards the Word of the Lord, the nation is subject to judgment. The Bible says that judgment of a nation can be averted:

"If I shut up heaven that there be no rain, or if I command the locusts to devour the land, or if I send pestilence among my people; If my people, which are called by my name, shall humble themselves, and pray, and seek my face, and turn from their wicked ways; then will I hear from heaven, and will forgive their sin, and will heal their land. Now mine eyes shall be open, and mine ears attend unto the prayer that is made in this place." (2 Chronicles 7:13-15)

There is a principle in place. Proverbs14:34 says, "Righteousness exalts a nation, but sin is a disgrace to any people." If we sin as a nation it is a disgrace to us as a people, but when we obey the Lord and fulfill all righteousness, we shall be exalted as a nation.

In 2 Chronicles, God is speaking to Solomon at the time that he is building the Temple. The place of reference in Scripture is Solomon's Porch. As we have seen previously, Solomon's Porch was known as the place where the women prayed. This has both a natural and a spiritual reference as a Prophetic Gate to the nation. God says, *"Now mine eyes shall be open, and mine ears attend unto the prayer that is made in this place". (2 Chronicles 7:13-15)*

He is talking about the Gate of a nation. God will meet us at the Gates of Entry and the Gates of Exit. This is what the Prayer Watch times represent.

The healing of the lame man that took place at the Beautiful Gate in Acts chapter 3 represented the entrance of The Healer to the Nation of Israel. God says, *"then will I hear from heaven, and will forgive their sin, and will heal their land."* Revival is God's Healing for a nation.

When a nation is spiritually dry and revelation is no longer flowing, the nation will enter apostasy and the effects can be catastrophic. It has the potential to destroy entire generations and create spiritual gaps that displace men and push them out of position. Without men in position, a nation will lose its identity. Nations fail and cease to exist when they lose their identity.

The Rise and Fall of Nations

History tells us that a nation either fails and ceases to exist or rises and is birthed when it loses or gains three things:

1. Its own language – its speech or its common dialect;

2. Its unique culture – the moral compass and a standard of behavior which is practiced in whole by its members; and
3. Its identity – which others can see and clearly identify the nation's members.

If these three things happen that nation must then experience one of two things:

1. Rebellion; or

2. Revival

The Kingdom of God is a nation in the Earth. The universal Church of Christ represents the

Kingdom of God. Not any singular denomination of Christianity, but the Church in the Earth is God's representation of the Kingdom of God. In Matthew 16, Peter gets the Revelation that Jesus Christ is the Son of God and Jesus tells him:

"And I say also unto thee, That thou art Peter, and upon this rock I will build my church; and the gates of hell shall not prevail against it." (Matthew 16:18)

The Church in some nations has lost its language. We are supposed to speak what the Spirit says; instead we are speaking like the world.

The Church in some nations has lost its culture. Churches are being populated by social media and marketing skills to fill up a building instead of preaching the Gospel message of Jesus Christ, born of a virgin, crucified on a cross, raised from the dead, went up to Heaven and will return again to judge the living and the dead.. God is not building your Kingdom. He is building His Kingdom. He is not building bricks and mortar to populate notable cities on Earth, but He is building men and women to populate the Kingdom of Heaven.

The Church in some nations is indeed suffering an identity crisis. Christians are debating issues that were settled in Genesis. Some churches are issue driven instead of Christ centered. Often, when you walk into the Church you will not be able to tell the difference between the Church and the World. We cannot be like them if we are going to ask them to come out of the Dark into the Light. If you are practicing your sin, you cannot also be a practicing Christian. Christianity is a discipline that trains Disciples of Christ. The Church is called to be the Ecclesia. Separated. Set Apart.

We need Revival!

The Church in the Earth is witnessing the uprising. The Rebellion of the World is spreading like wildfire without the Voice of the Church. The four Pillars of Society - The Church, The Government, Business and Family are all experiencing the effects of evil.

Only the Church can turn the tide. Only the Church can summon the assistance of Elohim and set in motion - A Revival. God, send the Revival. Rend the Heavens and Send the Revival!

When Israel entered the state of apostasy in epic proportions, God told Jeremiah to call for the wailing women. Jeremiah 9:17-21 says,

"Thus saith the Lord of hosts, Consider ye, and call for the mourning women, that they may come; and send for cunning women, that they may come: And let them make haste, and take up a wailing for us, that our eyes may run down with tears, and our eyelids gush out with waters. For a voice of wailing is heard out of Zion, How are we spoiled! we are greatly confounded, because we have forsaken the land, because our dwellings have cast us out. Yet hear the word of the Lord, O ye women, and let your ear receive the word of his mouth, and teach your daughters wailing, and every one her neighbour lamentation. For death is come up into our windows, and is entered into our palaces, to cut off the children from without, and the young men from the streets."

If we are going to stop the bloodshed that takes black lives, white lives, blue lives and is an infringement on all life – we are going to have to call for the Mothers, the Daughters, the Sisters – the Wailing Women – who will lift up a lamentation and make a proclamation before the courts of Elohim to release the Hand of God and bring the Healing Waters to the nation.

We must pray to release those that are bound according to the judgment written in Isaiah 49:24-26. Even the lawful captive will go free if we pray.

"Shall the prey be taken from the mighty, or the lawful captive delivered? But thus saith the Lord, Even the captives of the mighty shall be taken away, and the prey of the terrible shall be delivered: for I will contend with him that contendeth with thee, and I will save thy children. And I will feed them that oppress thee with their own flesh; and they shall be drunken with their own blood, as with sweet wine: and all flesh shall know that I the Lord am thy Saviour and thy Redeemer, the mighty One of Jacob."

Men and women in nations must take on a "massa" - a burden of the Lord. We must enter times and seasons of travail to pray for our nations.

All of our nations need Revival. We need Global Revival. Please pray. Pray now. Pray earnestly. Pray with expectancy! Your voice may be silent in the halls of National Government - but don't be discouraged! It is your lamentation that can and will be heard in the Courts of Elohim. When your cry reaches the Heavens and the BURDEN becomes too much - He will answer and send us Help to BREAK the Yoke of Bondage. Let's get on our Prayer Watch and pray for Revival in our Nations!

Declaring the Opening of The Gates

It is by prayer that we open the Gates to nations. In the next chapters, you will learn about the Four Watches of the Day and Four Watches of the Night. You must decide which Watch you will pray, but understand that when you take your position, when you are consistent and when you are diligent – you will receive insight and revelation that will enable you to become a Prophetic Intercessor for the Lord in your nation.

"Thus says the LORD to His anointed, to Cyrus, whose right hand I have held-To subdue nations before him And loose the armor of kings, to open before him the double doors, So that the gates will not be shut: 'I will go before you and make the crooked places straight; I will break in pieces the gates of bronze and cut the bars of iron. I will give you the treasures of darkness and hidden riches of secret places, that you may know that I, the LORD, who call you by your name, Am the God of Israel. For Jacob My servant's sake" (Isaiah 45:1-4)

Prayer Points

- We command the release of the Watchmen and the Wailing Women of this Generation and all who have been captured and bound by demonic legions - We command them loosed and set free from demonic forces in the name of Jesus.

- We interrupt and arrest every demon of addictions deployed to destroy the lives of great Intercessors and the Wailing Women of this Generation – we command their unconditional release from drug addiction, nicotine addiction, alcohol addiction, pornographic addiction, food addiction, sleep addiction and all such addictions designed to destroy their body before they are able to complete their God-given assignment. Let it be arrested in the name of Jesus.

- We call for Divine Judgment against the demon working through the internet, the media, political and social institutions of this age – We block them and shut them down – We execute the judgment written in Isaiah 49:24-26 that decrees even the prey of the mighty and the lawful captive shall go free in the name of Jesus.

- We shut down all their ability to contaminate and destroy The Righteous and the seed of The Righteous

- We command the release of the righteous and break their chains, we release them from the influence of demonic powers through the Superior Sacrifice of the Blood of Jesus.

- We destroy demonic strongholds in The Church and we destroy and uproot satanic footholds planted in the seed of The Righteous in the name of Jesus.

- We release the seven-fold spirits of God over The Righteous and The Seed of The Righteous in Jesus name.

- We command the release of angelic reinforcements and we decree angelic assistance for The Righteous in the name of Jesus.

- We overturn every time-sensitive plan of the enemy to destroy us at any gates of decision, gates of authority, gates of blessing in the name of Jesus.

- We interrupt and cancel satanic agendas and demonic programming to hurt us, our children, our families, our church, our leaders, our nation in the name of Jesus.

- We arrest demonic cartels, witches, warlocks, spirits without bodies or anyone who has sold themselves to the enemy in order to bring us pain, hurt, misfortune or cause us to fail in our God-given assignment in the name of Jesus.

- We break every hold of witchcraft, witchcraft assignments, and demonic agendas using a past or present mistake to exact vengeance on our glorious future in the name of Jesus.

- We release the Fire of God to confront and expose witchcraft projections, satanic agendas and all who devise our destruction. Let the opposite occur in the name of Jesus.

- We command our unconditional release and total freedom in the name of Jesus.

- We command the opening of divine gates that have been shut to us, in the name of Jesus.

Confession

I declare the release of the divine helpers for my nation. Release Divine Helpers who will open our gates of elevation, uplifting and divine promotion in the name of Jesus. I decree that I will walk in the great and effectual doors that are opened before me by divine appointment and through the power of intercession. I declare that this year will be my best, most favorable, most successful year in my family, in my church, in my nation in the name of Jesus. From the Throne Room perspective, I am ready to confront and dispossess the enemy and possess my possessions in the name of Jesus. I will get on my Prayer Watch and I will not stop praying, believing, giving, walking in faith or hoping in glory in this year and I look forward to declaring the goodness of the Lord in the land of the living all year in the name of Jesus.

Chapter Seven

The Prayer Watches

There are eight Prayer Watches described in the Bible. In the next several chapters, we will breakdown the prayer watch times and the focus of prayer with prayer points for each Watch. When you are an Intercessor, it is important that you pray often and regularly. At different times and seasons in your life, you may find that your prayer watch time changes or you may need to pray at multiple strategic times a day or night. Every Watch has a significant and distinct purpose.

The Lord instructed the disciples to *watch and pray* for an hour:

"Then Jesus returned and found them sleeping. "Simon, are you asleep?" He asked, "Were you not able to keep watch for one hour? Watch and pray so that you will not enter into temptation. For the spirit is willing, but the body is weak." Again He went away and prayed, saying the same thing." (Mark 14:37-39)

The Bible says the Lord went away and prayed the same thing for one hour. If we will be

88

persistent and consistent in our prayers we will be satisfied with revelation knowledge and see the travail of our soul.

"He shall see of the travail of His soul, and shall be satisfied. By His knowledge shall My righteous Servant justify many, for He shall bear their iniquities." (Isaiah 53:11)

As Intercessors, our prayers must be regular and consistent.

"I have set watchmen on your walls, O Jerusalem; they shall never hold their peace day or night. You who make mention of the LORD, do not keep silent, and give Him no rest till He establishes and till He makes Jerusalem a praise in the earth." Isaiah 62:6-7 (NKJV)

Watch!

To **_watch_** means to look out; to peer into the distance; to investigate or get a new scope on something; to see an approaching danger and **warn** those endangered:

And there stood a watchman on the tower in Jezreel, and he spied the company of Jehu as he came, and said, I see a company. And Joram said, Take a horseman, and send to meet them, and let him say, Is it peace? So there went one on horseback to meet him, and said, Thus saith the king, Is it peace? And Jehu said, What hast thou to do with peace? Turn thee behind me. And the watchman told, saying, The messenger came to them, but he cometh not again. (2 Kings 9:17-18)

Here we see the watchman on the tower who had the assignment to see the enemy of the city approaching. His assignment caused him to receive further instructions and to be sent to deliver a message. When we become Spiritual Watchmen – Prophetic Intercessors – we too will receive advance knowledge of the movements of the enemy, instructions from on high and a message of deliverance to warn the nation, the city, the church, our families and all to whom God has assigned us, so that we can escape the snares and traps of the wicked.

We are informed that the Proverbs 31 woman *"looketh well"* or *watches over* her household diligently, which means to see with advanced knowledge to ensure the future is secure.

"She looketh well to the ways of her household, and eateth not the bread of idleness." (Proverbs 31:27)

When we watch over our household and pray regularly for our spouses and our children, we will not be idle and we will take decisions that help secure the destiny of generations yet unborn.

We have already discussed why it is important to pray with advanced knowledge. When you pray regularly and you are persistent, God will show you revelation that will help you see the answer to your prayers. The Prayer Watch times help us to pray effectively during strategic times when we must be alert to avoid the wiles of the enemy.

The word "*shaqad*" means to be alert - to be wakeful, so you can see either for good or evil. The Lord expects us to be alert so that He can instruct us in times of prayer:

"And it shall come to pass, that like as I have watched over them, to pluck up, and to break down, and to throw down, and to destroy, and to afflict; so will I watch over them, to build, and to plant, saith the Lord. (Jeremiah 31:28)

We cannot be routine and familiar in our dealings with the Lord or with the enemy. When we watch and pray, we will not make assumptions and we will know when God is moving us to deploy new weapons and new strategies.

He wants us to be vigilant (alert) and build ourselves during times of prayer:

"Set up the standard upon the walls of Babylon, make the watch strong, set up the watchmen, prepare the ambushes: for the Lord hath both devised and done that which he spake against the inhabitants of Babylon." (Jeremiah 51:12)

We must be vigilant because the enemy is relentless and is maintaining a watch against us in the infernal realm. The Bible says to pray without ceasing (1 Thessalonians 5:17) because even when we may believe we have other things to do besides pray, we must know that the enemy has nothing else to do besides prey on us. Therefore we must be strategic and issue counter decrees against the decrees of the enemy. When we are alert we will not be ignorant of the devices of the enemy and we will cut off those who wait for our downfall.

"For the terrible one is brought to nought, and the scorner is consumed, and all that watch for iniquity are cut off." (Isaiah 29:20)

God sets up Intercessors over regions, nations, cities, churches, families, etc. Intercessors are called to *"shamar"* (to "protect") during a Day or Night Watch. We must be prepared as in the example in 2 Kings 11:5-7:

"And he commanded them, saying, This is the thing that ye shall do; A third part of you that enter in on the sabbath shall even be keepers of the watch of the king's house; And a third part shall be at the gate of Sur; and a third part at the gate behind the guard: so shall ye keep the watch of the house, that it be not broken down. And two parts of all you that go forth on the Sabbath, even they shall keep the watch of the house of the Lord about the king."

God is asking us to be stewards over a Watch against the enemy for our protection so that we will not be penetrated and have our gates broken down. The Watch Times are <u>Gates of Exit</u> and <u>Gates of Entry</u>. It is during these times that we are capable of disarming the forces of darkness operating against us.

"Nevertheless we made our prayer unto our God, and set a watch against them day and night, because of them." (Nehemiah 4:9)

It is during the Watch that God gives us strategies that help us remove the trusted weapons of our enemies. When we see the nation is under siege, it is the time for us to institute a Watch and be more vigilant to enforce the plan of God for our nation as in Nehemiah:

"And I said unto them, Let not the gates of Jerusalem be opened until the sun be hot; and while they stand by, let them shut the doors, and bar them: and appoint watches of the inhabitants of Jerusalem, every one in his watch, and every one to be over against his house." (Nehemiah 7:3)

When Jesus was on Earth, He pulled away to pray and kept Watch and warned the disciples to do the same. He warned them to Watch using the word *"gregoreo"* (to "keep awake, to watch") which in the Greek language means to "take heed, lest through remissiveness and indolence one be led to forsake Christ":

Watch and pray, that ye enter not into temptation: the spirit indeed is willing, but the flesh is weak. (Matthew 26:41)

Watch ye and pray, lest ye enter into temptation. The spirit truly is ready, but the flesh is weak. (Mark 14:38)

We can miss the move of God if we are not alert and willing to forfeit times of sleep and slumber to seek the Will of God.

Apostle Paul warned the early church to be vigilant and prayerful. The word *"nepho"* used in the New Testament means to "abstain from wine, be sober". Figuratively it means to be calm and collected in spirit; to be temperate, dispassionate, circumspect. We would not rely on emotions or external appearances if we learn to practice walking in the Spirit in times of prayer.

"Therefore let us not sleep, as do others; but let us watch and be sober." (1 Thessalonians 5:6)

The word *"nepho"* is the same word Paul used to advise Timothy on how to handle his ministry:

"But watch thou in all things, endure afflictions, do the work of an evangelist, make full proof of thy ministry." (2 Timothy 4:5).

Prayer Watch Times

In the Bible, we find a pattern. Watchmen were on the wall watching for the enemy and announcing what they saw. Again, when we see Watchmen, as it relates to prayer – we are talking about both male and female Intercessors. Matthew chapter 24:43 says:

"But know this, that if the good man of the house had known in what watch the thief would come, he would have watched, and would not have suffered his house to be broken up."

There are specific times we should be on our watch to deal effectively with the thief that comes to steal, kill and destroy. If we will be on our watch we will avert destruction in our nations, our cities, our churches and our families.

When we are able to watch, we will understand the time of visitation of the Lord. Jesus wept over the nation because they were unaware of the time of His visitation:

"And when he drew near and saw the city, he wept over it, saying, "Would that you, even you, had known on this day the things that make for peace! But now they are hidden from your eyes. For the days will come upon you, when your enemies will set up a barricade around you and surround you and hem you in on every side and tear you down to the ground, you and your children within you. And they will not leave one stone upon another in you, because you did not know the time of your visitation." (Luke 19:41-44)

If you do not Watch and Pray, you will not recognize the enemy when he approaches and you will suffer damages that could have been averted if only you had been alert during the time of Visitation. The enemy wants to scatter and destroy us when we are ignorant of his devices. It is during the eight watches of the day and night that we are able to gain access and an advantage over the power of darkness.

In the next chapters we will enforce the prophetic decrees of the various Prayer Watch times. The windows of time have specific Biblical purposes, which you should understand so that you can be more effective and strategic in your prayers. We will break each Watch in the following chapters, but listed below is an overview of the various watch times and their purposes.

Overview of the Eight Watches

1. **First Watch of the Day (or the Late Morning Watch): 6 a.m. to 9 a.m.:** – This time is for declarations and utterances, and a time when Divinity meets Humanity. This is the first watch of the day. This is the watch for the beginning of sunrise.

2. **Second Watch of the Day (the Exit and Entry Watch): 9 a.m. to Noon:** – This Watch is a time for forgiveness and healing, and is commonly referred to as the "Exits and Entry Watch". Intercessors should take advantage of this watch and pray to secure the gates.

3. **Third Watch of the Day (The Fullness of Day): Noon to 3 p.m.:** – The Third Watch of the Day is Noon to 3pm. This is a time where the preparation and work of the first two watches has the potential to bring explosive growth, financial increase and miraculous fulfillment to the Body of Christ.

4. **Fourth Watch of the Day (The Transformation Watch): 3 p.m. to 6 p.m.**: – This Watch is the time to transform history and remove veils; this is the time when the veil was torn that we may receive access to the Father through Jesus Christ our mediator. (Matthew 27:45-53).

5. **First Watch of the Night (The Early Night Watch): 6 p.m. to 9 p.m.**: – This is a critical hour to command the release of financial blessings. This is a natural and a Spiritual Gate and it is important to command the new (next) day from the declarations made on this Watch..

6. **Second Watch of the Night (The Late Night Watch) 9pm to Midnight:** – This is a time for thanksgiving and solemn preparation for the Third Watch of the Night.

7. **Third Watch of the Night (The Warfare Watch) Midnight to 3 a.m.**: –The Third Watch of the Night is one of the most important Watches. Midnight is a very strategic Watch and is symbolic of intense darkness; but God is the light in the darkness and releases divine strategy

during this time. It is the time in which spiritual warfare takes place and where satanic activities are at its height, hence why it is commonly referred to as the Warfare watch.

8. **The Fourth Watch of the Night (The Morning Watch) 3 a.m. to 6 a.m.:** – This Watch is a time to pray for freedom of the Church. This Watch is the time when God releases the dew and blessings of heaven.

The Watch is a Spiritual Gate

These eight watches of the Day and Night are Spiritual Gates. As an Intercessor, it is important to realize that your role is that of a gatekeeper. Through prayers of intercession, you are standing watch over the gates and walls of your nations, your cities, your churches, your families, etc. Your role is very critical in spiritual warfare and strategic prayer to break through the resistance of the enemy and allow the illumination of God's Light and the Fires of Revival to affect this generation and the generations yet unborn. Your prayers are powerful!

Gates, walls and gatekeepers can have meaning from a defensive position (protecting something from an enemy) or offensive position (storming the enemies gates or walls). Nations can have these, cities can have these, regions can have them, houses can have them, churches can have them, and people (individuals) can have them. When Peter healed the lame man (Acts chapter 3), it was done at the Gate Beautiful and the church grew to 5000 that day. If we will go behind the scenes and dismantle the strongman sitting over the destiny of our nations, cities, families, etc. we will see the greatest move of God in our day and time. We can do it if we are willing and obedient to Watch and Pray during strategic times on a regular basis.

Prayer Points

- By the grace made available through the superior sacrifice of the Lord Jesus, we enforce favorable conditions and that the atmosphere over our gates is conducive for us to hear from God the strategies that will defeat the strongman sitting over our destiny and the future of our nation in the name of Jesus.

- We decree that we will be endowed with power from on High to pray fervent prayers and that as we keep coming to God, He will keep increasing our fire power to give us new weapons in prayer that will disarm the enemy and give us total victory in the name of Jesus.

- We cancel any assignment of the enemy that has been set in motion to disfavor us or bring us to shame and disgrace in the name of Jesus.

- We enforce our set time of favor to overrule any satanic pregnancies or witchcraft agendas designed to deny, delay or hinder our day or night that we have determined to seek the Lord while He may be found, we will not be distracted in the name of Jesus.

- We declare that wherever we are, whatever we do, we will commit and stay committed to complete times of prayer and fasting that break every resistance of the enemy and set men and women free in our nations, our cities and our families in the name of Jesus.

- We deprogram all satanic programming to put us to sleep and cause the spirit of slumber to come over us when it is time for us to be alert, awake and watchful in the name of Jesus. We will be alert, aware and vigilant in Jesus name.

- We deploy the angels of the Lord and the Host of Heaven to bring illumination to hidden agendas of darkness and to increase the vision of gatekeepers, doorkeepers, key holders and people in strategic positions to favor the righteous and the seed of the righteous in the name of Jesus.

Confession

From today, I will stand upon my watch and wait for the revelation of the Lord to have keys for the issues of my life, my nation, my city, my family, etc. In the name of Jesus, I will deploy the key of revelation to open doors, to access gates and to unseat my enemies. By revelation I possess keys that will expose witchcraft assignments and overturn satanic gatherings in the name of Jesus. By the key of Divine Illumination I will escape wicked traps and satanic pitfalls in the name of Jesus. It is by these keys that the counsel of the wicked is discovered and the devices of the crafty are overturned in the name of Jesus. Lord, the closer I come, continue to speak to me by Revelation and release to me new keys, in the name of Jesus. Amen.

Chapter Eight

The First Watch of the Day

Pray for the Strengthening of the Five-Fold Ministry

Prayers must be made to see the release and strengthening of those who are called to the Five-Fold ministry. The Bible says, Prayers must be consistent and persistent. Before Jesus came to Earth, someone had to pray. The Bible says in the book of Luke that Simeon "was waiting for the consolation of Israel" and was filled with the Spirit and had received by revelation a Word that he would not die until the Messiah came.

"And, behold, there was a man in Jerusalem, whose name was Simeon; and the same man was just and devout, waiting for the consolation of Israel: and the Holy Ghost was upon him. And it was revealed unto him by the Holy Ghost, that he should not see death, before he had seen the Lord's Christ. And he came by the Spirit into the temple: and when the parents brought in the child Jesus, to do for him after the custom of the law, Then took he him up in his arms, and blessed God, and said, Lord, now lettest thou thy servant depart in peace, according to thy word:

For mine eyes have seen thy salvation, Which thou hast prepared before the face of all people; A light to lighten the Gentiles, and the glory of thy people Israel. And Joseph and his mother marvelled at those things that were spoken of him. And Simeon blessed them, and said unto Mary his mother, Behold, this child is set for the fall and rising again of many in Israel; and for a sign which shall be spoken against; (Yea, a sword shall pierce through thy own soul also,) that the thoughts of many hearts may be revealed." (Luke 2:25-35)

Someone in this generation has been born to be relevant in the Kingdom of God and to bless the people of God. God will release those called to the five-fold ministry for the building of the Church and to set the captives free in every generation. But, nothing happens until somebody prays. This generation must live for a cause greater than themselves and take care to speak and release the future of the next generation. We must pray in this generation to release and strengthen the five-fold ministry giftings.

Enforce The First Watch of the Day: 6am-9am Prayer Watch

Overturn Satanic Verdicts, Rulings and Judgments Against the Five-Fold Ministry and the Body of Christ

First Watch of the Day (or the Late Morning Watch): 6 a.m. to 9 a.m. – This time is for declarations and utterances; equipment of service; transforming of minds; the time that God strengthens Christians. Jesus was crucified at 9am or the Third Hour of the Day. The Holy Spirit came before the Third Hour (which is between 8am and 9am). God saw fit to mention this time in the Bible as a time of great significance for Divinity to have a point of contact with Humanity. This is the first watch of the day. This is the watch for the beginning of sunrise.

Scriptures to Meditate on and Things to Pray For:

Healing
Study Scriptures: Malachi 4:2-3; Acts 10:38

Outpouring of The Holy Spirit
Study Scriptures: Matthew 3:16-17; Luke 4:1; Acts 2:1-21

The Gifts of The Spirit To Manifest

Study Scriptures: Luke 11:13; Acts 2:1-4; Acts 2:17-18

Divine Illumination of God's Word

Study Scriptures: Psalm 43:3; Proverbs 4:18; John 11:9-10; Matthew 5:14-16; Romans 13:12

The Gospel to Have Free Course and Be Effective

Study Scriptures: John 14:15-29; John 16:12-14; John 15:26; Ephesians 1:13

Prayer Points

- By the Power of the Holy Spirit and through the Blood of Jesus, I will rise early in the morning and decree my day shall be filled with good success and I will not fail in the name of Jesus

- I release the work of my hands, the movement of my feet and the strength of my mind to overcome all the tactics, plans and schemes of the enemy that may face me throughout this new day the Lord has made in the name of Jesus.

- I dismantle, uproot and overturn all the conceptions and programming of the wicked that have been projected into the womb of time for this day. I discover, deprogram and destroy all such wicked programmings in the name of Jesus.

- I overturn satanic verdicts, rulings and judgments against the five-fold Ministry and the Body of Christ

- Let every plan of the enemy to destroy the life, hinder the work or oppose the advancement of those called to the five-fold ministry be uncovered, uprooted and overturned in the name of Jesus

- Let the plans of the enemy to interrupt and subvert the release of those called to the five-fold ministry that was consumed and set in motion in the night be aborted in the name of Jesus.

- Let the judgment written in Hosea 9:14 be deployed against the wicked. Give them a dry breast and a miscarrying womb in the name of Jesus. Whatever they have planned for the righteous and the seed of the righteous, it shall not stand, it shall not come to pass and I command it to overturn now in the name of Jesus!

- I reveal and uncover by the Blood of Jesus every spirit that operates behind the scenes, every disembodied spirit that uses those that are close to me, even my own family, co-workers, relationships, friends or anyone who has opened themselves up to be used by the devil to destroy, contaminate or subvert my glorious future or the future of anyone else who is called to the five-fold ministry. I command our unconditional release now in the name of Jesus.

- Let such plans of the wicked, schemes of the enemy and wiles of the devil be exposed and let those plans fail in the name of Jesus.

- I block all wicked access to my nation, my leaders, myself, my children, and anyone who is called to the five-fold ministry or who is called to favor the cause of the righteous, let all access of the wicked be blocked in the name of Jesus!

- I overturn satanic verdicts and witchcraft projections for terrorism and destruction that have been programmed into the womb of time for this day. Let them be revealed, averted, located and dismantled in the name of Jesus.

- I call for the Fire of God to locate, expose and destroy every snake and scorpion that is operating behind the scenes in my nation, my city, my church, my family, my workplace or my life in the name of Jesus. Let any such wickedness catch fire now in the name of Jesus.

- I cancel every appointment with disappointment, failure and denial that was programmed into today – let it be canceled in the name of Jesus

- By the superior power of the Blood of Jesus, I release total victory and the power to overcome and do great exploits into this new day in the name of Jesus.

Confession

I will live and not die today. I will prosper and see the goodness of the Lord in the land of the living. Just as I have crossed over the night, I will cross over the day and enter the next day with total victory. No hurt, harm or danger will befall me, my children, my nation, the church, and those called to the five-fold ministry, in the workplace, in the marketplace or anywhere we are located today. We have Divine Immunity and Supernatural Protection as Angels are released to cover our footsteps and ensure that no strange accidents, weird incidents or wicked manipulations come near us, our children, our loved ones, the seed of the righteous or anyone we must travel with today. By prayer, I take a comprehensive divine insurance policy on all modes of transportation, drivers, pilots, engineers, by water, by air, on the highways and by-ways, however the righteous travel today – let it be covered by the Blood of Jesus. We take a comprehensive divine insurance policy through the Blood of Jesus and command Angels to provide guidance and protection throughout this day. By prayer and intercession I release the fruitfulness of this day and deploy Goodness and Mercy to follow us throughout this day. Thank You Lord for helping us to achieve all that You have for us to do in this day. Thank You for Divine Provision and the Supernatural Release of

Favor. We will be strengthened today and You will use us to release Revival. Thank You Lord!

Chapter Nine

The Second Watch of the Day

Pray For This Generation of Intercessors

In the book of Luke we learn there was a Prophetess named Anna who "never left the temple, but prayed there night and day" until she saw the Messiah:

And there was one Anna, a prophetess, the daughter of Phanuel, of the tribe of Aser: she was of a great age, and had lived with an husband seven years from her virginity; And she was a widow of about fourscore and four years, which departed not from the temple, but served God with fasting and prayer night and day. And she coming in that instant gave thanks likewise unto the Lord, and spake of him to all them that looked for redemption in Jerusalem. (Luke 2:36-38)

Prophetess Anna was dedicated to prayer daily. She was consistent and persistent. For eighty-four years as a widow, she prayed. When she saw the travail of her soul, this widow woman went out and evangelized and *"spake of him to all them that looked for redemption in Jerusalem"*. She was not just concerned for her generation, but she showed concern for the next generation. She was faithful until the end. That is what God expects of all of us when we take our position as Intercessors. Let us watch and pray.

Enforce The Second Watch of the Day
9am-Noon Prayer Watch

Pray for Divine Preservation and Protection of This Generation and the Next Generation of Intercessors

Second Watch of the Day (the Exit and Entry Watch): 9 a.m. to Noon – Jesus was crucified at 9 a.m. (Matthew 15:25). He said, "It is finished" (John 19:30). Once He finished the work of the Cross; He was able to go down and take captivity captive. At Calvary, He was able to set the captives free and release the five-fold ministry gifts and mantles (Ephesians 4). This is a time for forgiveness; healing of relationships; harvest; scientific and technological advances. This is known as the "Exits and Entry Watch". This is the time most people begin their work. But, if we are going to be effective, we must have made some sacrifices and declarations before we begin our day. We must exit the Night and enter the

Day having taken a decision to take captivity captive and to release the blessings of the Day.

Scriptures to Meditate on and Things to Pray For:

For the Glory of God to be Revealed
Study Scriptures: 1 Kings 18

For God's Daily Promises to Be Fulfilled
Study Scriptures: 1 Kings 8:56; Joshua 23:14; Matthew 6:9-15

For The Work of Your Hands to be Supplied (all looking for a job)
Study Scriptures: Matthew 20:3-9; Psalm 90:17; Proverbs 3:4, Ecclesiastes 9:10

That You Will Not Be Idle
Study Scriptures: Acts 2:15; Colossians 3:5; Ephesians 4:28; Proverbs 19:15; 2 Thessalonians 3:11

For the Plans of the Wicked to Fail and The Righteous to be Elevated
Study Scriptures: 1 Kings 18:25-28, Esther 6

To Live a Crucified Life in Christ

Study Scriptures: Matt. 10:38-39; Galatians 2:20; Colossians 3:2-11; Galatians 5:19-21

Release the Harvest of God

Study Scriptures: Matthew 9:35-38; Acts 2:40-42

For the Preservation and Protection of This Generation and the Next Generation

Study Scriptures: Colossians 2:13-15; Esther 9; Nehemiah 9

Prayer Points

- By the Supreme Sacrifice of the Blood of Jesus, we overrule, override and overturn demonic predictions, handwriting and ordinances contrary to the preservation and protection of this generation and the next generation in the name of Jesus.

- We cancel the judgment written against this generation and the next generation by demonic handwritings in the name of Jesus.

- We release Mercy and the Voice of the Blood of Jesus over every contrary voice crying out against this generation in the name of Jesus.

- By the Supreme Sacrifice of the Blood of Jesus, we overrule, override and overturn the consequences of past actions, errors, and mistakes made through ignorance of the manipulations and calculations of the powers of the Dark Kingdom that are being held in satanic vaults to be used against the next generation in the name of Jesus.

- We command Divine Escapes and Deliverance for the seed of the righteous and generations yet unborn in the name of Jesus.

- We decree the seed of The Righteous shall not perish, but shall be delivered in the name of Jesus.

- By the Supreme Sacrifice of the Blood of Jesus, we interrupt, override and overturn the weapon of premature and untimely death against the children of God, the men and women of God in this generation and the next generation in the name of Jesus.

- We decree long life and lengthening of days for The Righteous and the household of The Righteous in the name of Jesus.

- We decree Divine Preservation for The Righteous in the name of Jesus.

- We secure the Harvest of The Righteous and the inheritance for the seed of The Righteous in the name of Jesus.

- We block all demonic openings in the life of The Righteous and the seed of the Righteous in this generation and the next generation in the name of Jesus.

- We deny the demonic world access to The Righteous and the seed of the Righteous in this generation and the next generation in the name of Jesus. This generation will not pervert the justice of the Lord and will lift up a lamentation for the next generation to secure Divine Destinies now in the name of Jesus.

- We command the outpouring of the spirit of Grace and Intercession to come on The Church now in the name of Jesus.

- We decree community transformation to come over nations now in the name of Jesus.

- We break the curse of bewitchment and the spell of spiritual blindness now in the name of Jesus.

- We decree the recovery of sight, the release of the gifts of miracles and fresh empowerment from the Holy Spirit to overtake The Church and The Intercessors in this generation and the next generation now in the name of Jesus.

Confession

I will not be idle and will let the works of my hands be dedicated to the work of the Lord regardless of whether I am a worker in my family house, in the marketplace or in the House of God. I will be diligent, dedicated and prepared to give my time and attention in the Spirit of Excellence to whatever God has assigned me to do in the Earth. I repent for wasted seed, wasted years, wasted time, wasted opportunities and anything that does not represent me taking full advantage of every opportunity God has given me to be more than a conqueror and a total overcomer in the world. I will enter new heights, walk through open doors and possess my possessions in this generation. I will not be a bad example to the next generation but I will teach them by example how to serve the Lord and fulfill the plans of God to destroy the works of darkness in the name of Jesus. Help me Lord to be relevant and successful in the age I have been born and to leave a mark for good and not for evil in the name of Jesus.

Chapter Ten

The Third Watch of the Day

Invoke Divine Immunity By The Blood Of Jesus
Over The Movements Of God's Children

The Bible says that when you dwell in the
"secret place of the Most High" you have this
promise:

*"You shall not be afraid of the terror by night,
Nor of the arrow that flies by day, Nor of the
pestilence that walks in darkness, Nor of the
destruction that lays waste at noonday." (Psalm
91:5-6)*

That is a promise that concerns the Watches
and what the assignment of the enemy is to
oppose you during times and seasons of the
Day and Night Watches. The enemy will
attempt to bring "destruction that lays waste
at noonday". But, if you will purpose to be on
your Watch, you can preempt the plan of the
enemy and break every resistance to the
advancement of the Kingdom of God.

Apostle Paul was traveling along with Silas
and Timothy and they desired and longed to

visit the Church in Thessalonica. But the Bible says in 1 Thessalonians 2:18:

"Wherefore we would have come unto you, even I Paul, once and again; but Satan hindered us."

Even though they truly wanted to accomplish the mission, it was impossible because of the resistance. We must not be ignorant of the devices of Satan. Apostle Paul faced resistance from Satan, even though he had already described his love for the work and his prayers for the Church he had planted in Thessalonica when he described this particular church in 1 Thessalonians 1:2-3:

"We give thanks to God always for you all, making mention of you in our prayers: remembering without ceasing your work of faith, and labor of love, and patience of hope in our Lord Jesus Christ, in the sight of God and our Father."

The will of Paul was overruled as to him personally visiting the church, so he had to send Timothy alone to minister and hold the church together until he could break the resistance of Satan to permit him to come and attend to their needs personally.

This satanic resistance was not the same as the resistance and redirection of the Holy Spirit. The Bible says in Acts 16:6-7:

"Now when they had gone throughout Phrygia and the region of Galatia, and were forbidden of the Holy Ghost to preach the word in Asia, After they were come to Mysia, they assayed to go into Bithynia: but the Spirit suffered them not."

The resistance of Satan was not the same as the redirection of the Holy Spirit. This kind of resistance has to do with a power struggle between two kingdoms. This kind of resistance must be broken by a battle in prayer. We must intercede to break satanic resistance that comes to scatter the work, monitor the growth or waste the blessings of God's children.

The Words *"Satan hindered them"* means that Satan concerned himself with their movements and attempted to hinder or block them in order to scatter and break the Thessalonian Church. Too often today we are ignorant of the devices of Satan and we permit his resistance to cause work done in one generation that advances the Church, to be wasted in the next generation and the enemy is able to take back territory that was not defended in prayer. We must spend this hour of the Watch destroying the resistance of Satan and commanding invisible barriers to the End-Time Harvest to fall.

Let's Watch and Pray.

Enforce The Third Watch of the Day
Noon – 3pm Prayer Watch

Command Invisible Barriers to the End-Time Harvest to Fall

Pray for Fruitfulness in the Kingdom of God

Third Watch of the Day (The Fullness of Day): Noon to 3 p.m. – The Third Watch of the Day is Noon to 3pm. This is a time where the preparation and work of the first two watches has the potential to bring explosive growth, financial increase and miraculous fulfillment to the Body of Christ. Even in your personal life, what you are able to accomplish in the early morning has the potential to begin yielding fruit in this Watch. This is also the time that Satan and his infernal kingdom attempt to hinder, waste, scatter and block the life of God's people, the Church and the Harvest of God in our lives. This is the time that Satan comes to destroy any advancement previously made in the Kingdom of God.

This is the prayer watch that introduces the Midday, Noon, the Sixth Hour or the Fullness of Day. This is the time that the sun is at its fullest, and should yield its optimum best. It is a time for the shaking of foundations and judgment. It is a time for fruitfulness and in the gathering of the Harvest. It is a time for divine guidance and for deliverance from evil and wickedness.

Scriptures to Meditate on and Things to Pray For:

The Fulfillment of Prophecy and the Overturning of Generational Curses
Study Scriptures: Hosea 7:1; John 4:6 (The Revival of Samaria); Genesis 49:19; Mark 5:1-20 (The Man of Gaderenes)

Let The Wickedness of the Wicked to Come to an End
Study Scriptures: Matthew 27:45; Acts 26:13; Psalm 7:9; Psalm 10:15

Release the Spoiler and the Plunderer to Waste the Waster
Study Scriptures: Isaiah 54:15-17; Jeremiah 15:8

Release the Glory of the Lord Over the Righteous and Failure for the Wicked
Study Scriptures: Job 11:13-20; Deuteronomy. 28:7; Proverbs 28:1; Psalm 53:5

That You Will Abide in the Secret Place of the Most High
Study Scriptures: Psalm 91:1-8

Fulfill Your Daily Purpose and Release Fruitfulness
Study Scriptures: Proverbs 4:18; Psalm 1:3; Jeremiah 17:8; Leviticus 26:4

Pray Against Destruction That Strikes at Noonday
Study Scriptures: Psalm 91:6-7

Destroy Invisible Barriers and Satanic Resistance
Study Scriptures: Isaiah 25:7; Lamentations 3:44; 2 Corinthians 3:14-16; 2 Corinthians 4:3-5; Genesis 21:16-19

Destroy Spiritual Blindness

Study Scriptures: Ephesians 1:16-19; 1
Corinthians 2:7-12; John
12:39-41; Romans 11:7-10;
Jeremiah 5:21; Psalm 115:5-
6; Psalm 135:16-18

Prayer Points

- We uproot the plantings of the enemy in our nation, our cities, our churches, our families and our work places according to what is written in Matthew 15:13 in Jesus' name. Let whatever the Father has not planted and is being used to resist us, let it break now in the name of Jesus.

- In the name of Jesus, we unblock rivers of life and the Living Waters of The Righteous and the seed of The Righteous. Let the wells be unblocked so that there can be a free flow of the Gospel and the release of five-fold ministry giftings in the name of Jesus. Let Revival Waters flow.

- We override, overturn and overrule every injustice and wickedness against the church, The Righteous and the seed of The Righteous. Let those legislations and handwritings that are contrary to our progress and that are designed to cause the Church to move backward instead of forward – let the laws be overturned, overruled and denied in the name of Jesus.

- We break every legality and technicality that is being used as a trusted weapon of the enemy to destroy the work of our hands, the work of the Fathers and Mothers of the church, the advancement of the Kingdom of God in the Earth in this generation – let those trusted weapons be destroyed now in the name of Jesus.

- We arrest the spirit of heaviness in the life of The Righteous in Jesus name. We arrest the spirit of weariness that comes over The Righteous because of the hindrance of the enemy. We release a fresh wind of power and strength to blow over The Righteous now in the name of Jesus. Do it again Oh Lord!

- By the Supreme Sacrifice of the Blood of Jesus, we overrule, override and overturn demonic demands for destruction, desires of Hell, Death and The Grave against The Righteous. Let the claims be denied in the name of Jesus.

- We arrest all the demands of premature death to take out Generals of the Faith in this Generation and to locate the seed of the Righteous for the next Generation. Let the appointment with Death, Hell and the Grave be canceled now in the name of Jesus.

- We will not bury any Intercessor called to pray for this Generation before their time. We decree they shall finish all their days and complete their mission healthy, wealthy and whole in the name of Jesus.

- We command every giant and beast – ancient devils – restricted to the place of Divine Appointment in the name of Jesus.

- We arrest the Spirit of Fear and Terror that is gripping this Generation through enemy tactics to intimidate The Righteous and silence their voice in the name of Jesus. We release the Spirit of the Lord to give them boldness to speak the Word in Season and set the captives free in the name of Jesus.

By the superior power of the Blood of Jesus, through deep intercession, different kinds and types of prayers and fasting; I move into the realm of the Spirit and resist the devil and demonic activity working against me, my family, community, my church and nation. I expose satanic agendas set in motion by altars, persons without bodies, witchcraft activities, the counsel of the wicked and mistakes of my past in the name of Jesus. I exercise tenacious faith and set up steadfast barriers of resistance opposing the plan of the devil through the keys of prayer, fasting, sacrifice and service in the House of God in the name of Jesus. Let my activities in the Spirit, my sacrifices for the Kingdom of God and my service in the House of God stand as a memorial and fortress against the schemes, plans and tactics of the devil in the name of Jesus. I release the arrow of God to preempt and cut off the arrows of Satan shot against me suddenly to cause me to fall from the Grace of God. Let the arrows be turned back now in the name of Jesus.

Chapter Eleven

The Fourth Watch of the Day

Pray Thy Kingdom Come

Satan's kingdom mandate is to be a cloud of confusion that hinders the original plan of God and prevents the Kingdom of God from being made manifest. That is why Jesus said in Luke 11:2 for us to pray "Thy Kingdom Come".

This Watch, the Fourth Watch, specifically 3pm is known in the Bible as the Hour of Prayer. It has a special significance because it marks the hour that Christ died on the Cross following a period of gross darkness:

"Now from the sixth hour there was darkness over all the land unto the ninth hour." (Matthew 27:45)

This Hour of Prayer is the Hour of Divine Access. The Bible says that after Jesus gave up His Life and died on the Cross-, the veil in the temple was rent in two:

"Then, behold, the veil of the temple was torn in two from top to bottom; and the earth quaked, and the rocks were split, and the graves were

opened; and many bodies of the saints who had fallen asleep were raised; and coming out of the graves after His resurrection, they went into the holy city and appeared to many." (Matthew 27:51-53)

It also marks the time that Peter and John healed the lame man at the Beautiful Gate (Acts 3:1) and 5000 men were added to the Church that day (Acts 4:4). Lastly, the Bible also records that this is the hour that a Gentile named Cornelius became the first of the Gentiles to receive Christ.

"There was a certain man in Caesarea called Cornelius, a centurion of what was called the Italian Regiment, a devout man and one who feared God with all his household, who gave alms generously to the people, and prayed to God always. About the ninth hour of the day he saw clearly in a vision an angel of God coming in and saying to him, "Cornelius!" (Acts 10:1-3)

Cornelius is a devout Gentile. He has gained access to God by his principles, but now he will gain access through the power of intercession. Intercessors are God's voice to enforce the Ordinances of Heaven in the Earth. Cornelius is instructed to go and see Peter. The Bible says in Acts 10:9-16 that Peter is praying at the sixth hour (noon) and sees in a vision God asking him to do something he had never done before:

"The next day, as they went on their journey and drew near the city, Peter went up on the housetop to pray, about the sixth hour. Then he became very hungry and wanted to eat; but while they made ready, he fell into a trance and saw heaven opened and an object like a great sheet bound at the four corners, descending to him and let down to the earth. In it were all kinds of four-footed animals of the earth, wild beasts, creeping things, and birds of the air. And a voice came to him, "Rise, Peter; kill and eat." But Peter said, "Not so, Lord! For I have never eaten anything common or unclean." And a voice spoke to him again the second time, "What God has cleansed you must not call common." This was done three times. And the object was taken up into heaven again."

Apostle Peter is the leader of the Early Church. He has been given the authority – the keys – to bind and loose (Matthew 16:19). He has Divine Access to Heaven. When Peter goes to meet Cornelius the next day, Cornelius has gathered his family and friends. The Bible says that Peter preached and prayed for Cornelius and his friends and this happened:

"While Peter was still speaking these words, the Holy Spirit fell upon all those who heard the word." (Acts 10:44)

Intercessors are the most powerful people on the Earth today. Intercessors are appointed for the purpose of bringing God into the affairs of men. God will not intervene, unless someone prays.

Let's Watch and Pray.

Enforce the Fourth Watch of the Day
3pm – 6pm Prayer Watch

Pray to Destroy the Wickedness of the Wicked and Reverse Satanic Verdicts

Fourth Watch of the Day (The Transformation Watch): 3pm to 6pm – Time to transform history; time to remove veils, coverings of darkness; prayer hour of covenants; the hour of triumphant glory; and the time for establishing The Kingdom. This is the time when Jesus was on the cross and said, "It is finished." At 3:00 pm Jesus gave up His Life in order that we might have access to Eternal

Life. After Jesus went through 6 hours of suffering for the deliverance of all mankind, the veil was torn that we may receive access to the Father through Jesus Christ our mediator. (Matthew 27:45-53). Jesus is our Great Intercessor. It is the power of Intercession that gives us access to Heaven. Through Intercession, we have authority to bring the Kingdom of Heaven to the Earth. We must pray "Thy Kingdom Come"!

It is only the Church in the Earth that has this authority. Scripture reveals that when Heaven is made manifest in the Earth, it is because of the *saints*. Our prayers have power to produce results on Earth. The one single most important characteristic or practice that identifies the church is prayer. The most important privilege of the entire church is prayer and the only hour in the Bible that is specifically referred to as the Hour of Prayer begins at 3:00 p.m. (Acts 3:1)

Scriptures to Meditate on and Things to Pray For:

Pray for Revelation, Grace And Removing All Limits

Study Scriptures: Matthew 27:45-53

Pray For Answered Prayers, Release of Miracles & Angelic Visitations
Study Scriptures: 1 Kings 18:25-39; Acts 10

Pray For Strategic Changes to Be Made That Favor the Righteous
Study Scriptures: Esther 9; Luke 23:45-47

Pray for Continued Access, Open Gates, Open Doors for the Righteous
Study Scriptures: Isaiah 60:11-22

Prayer Points

- Through the Blood of Jesus we overrule satanic verdicts designed to block the release of the End-Time Harvest in Jesus name.

- We decree and declare the establishment of His Kingdom and decree the will of God over families, communities, churches and cities in the name of Jesus.

- Through the power of the Blood of Jesus, we destroy satanic cartels and wicked strongholds that have become satanic horns that have wearied the Church and brought growth and advancement to a standstill in this generation. Let the embargoes be lifted and the opposition be broken in the name of Jesus.

- We release by Divine Authority divine helpers for the end-time harvest, the church, the body of Christ and the establishment of the five-fold ministry. We untie those who will help the church, help build the Kingdom, help the righteous and the seed of the righteous. Let them be untied now in the name of Jesus.

- We release the Grace of Salvation where there is a stronghold of the enemy preventing the free flow of the Gospel. We command the Gates be lifted so the King of Glory can come in. Let the Gates of Nations be lifted and the Doors of Access be opened in the Name of Jesus.

- We interrupt and destroy devices that are designed to operate, oppose and hinder the church and the five-fold ministry enforcing the judgment written in Ezekiel 11:2, 4, and 13. Let them be dismantled and let any wicked gatekeeper be arrested now in the name of Jesus.

- By the Supreme Sacrifice of the Blood of Jesus, we take possession of the gates of the enemy and secure the gates of The Righteous in the name of Jesus.

- We arrest every projection, inhibition, embargo and restriction of the wicked designed to manipulate, destroy, delay, deny or subvert the release of the End-time harvest in the name of Jesus. Let the Fire of God consume the wickedness of the wicked now in the name of Jesus.

- We call for the East Wind to quench strange fires and evil flames that prevent the advancement of the Gospel in the name of Jesus.

- Let the Kingdom of God have dominion and rulership over every other kingdom and wherever the Righteous dwells in this generation in the name of Jesus.

- Release supernatural testimonies, answers to prayer, sudden breakthroughs and notable miracles, signs and wonders in the Church to draw men to God and release Revival in this generation in the name of Jesus.

Confession:

In the name of Jesus I willingly submit my own
will, thoughts and intents to the will and
desire of Jehovah. Through the study of the
Word of God and through prayers,
intercession and fasting I seek to discover the
Will of God for the difficult situations of my
life. I will not lean to my own understanding,
but in all my ways I will acknowledge Him and
seek to know His counsel and plan for my life,
my family, my community, my church and my
nation in the name of Jesus. Even when it is
difficult and I am faced with temptations, I will
not give in or give out but I will stand on the
Word of God and place my faith in Christ Jesus
to overcome every temptation, test and trial
with the weapons He has provided for me to
be victorious in every area of my life in the
name of Jesus. I block and cut off the voice of
the enemy and satanic whisperings that seek
to make me error and not follow the voice of
God in the name of Jesus. I block those voices
now in the name of Jesus. I release the Voice of
the Blood of Jesus to overrule and override the
voice of any contrary wind seeking to blow me
off course from my divine destiny in the name
of Jesus.

Chapter Twelve

The First Watch of the Night

Understanding Gates and Keys

In Matthew 16:16-19, Jesus tells Peter that by revelation, he has gained access that will give him keys of authority to command Gates:

"Simon Peter answered and said, "You are the Christ, the Son of the living God." Jesus answered and said to him, "Blessed are you, Simon Bar-Jonah, for flesh and blood has not revealed this to you, but My Father who is in heaven. And I also say to you that you are Peter, and on this rock I will build My church, and the gates of Hades shall not prevail against it. And I will give you the keys of the kingdom of heaven, and whatever you bind on earth will be bound in heaven, and whatever you loose on earth will be loosed in heaven."

Hell has a Gate. Heaven also has a Gate. Time is filled with Gates of Access and Doors that open and Windows that close. Our day has a Gate, our week has a Gate, our month has a Gate and our year has a Gate. We must possess these gates, because whoever possesses the gates possesses and controls everything. What gives them power is when they hold the Key to exercise their Authority in Time. I can be the Gatekeeper, but I must recognize the Time in order to be effective. The very First Watch of the Night is the Gate to begin commanding the order of a New Day.

Examine Job 38:4-14:

"Where were you when I laid the foundations of the earth? Tell Me, if you have understanding. Who determined its measurements? Surely you know! Or who stretched the line upon it? To what were its foundations fastened? Or who laid its cornerstone, When the morning stars sang together, And all the sons of God shouted for joy? " (Job 38:4-7)

God is enquiring of Job and saying the earth has a foundation and measurements. But, He goes on to tell Him that even the sea has bars and doors:

"Or who shut in the sea with doors, When it burst forth and issued from the womb; When I made the clouds its garment, And thick darkness its swaddling band; When I fixed My limit for it, And set bars and doors; When I said,

'This far you may come, but no farther, And here your proud waves must stop!" (Job 38:8-11)

The Lord is describing the foundation of the earth and giving its restrictions and limitations. A good Intercessor is like a good defense attorney. The best defense attorney knows the law and understands the legalities and technicalities that prevent a conviction and that will cause even the lawful captive to be set free. Here God is giving Job secrets that can be used to navigate and command the even the elements to comply with the laws of Elohim:

"Have you commanded the morning since your days began, And caused the dawn to know its place, That it might take hold of the ends of the earth And the wicked be shaken out of it?" (Job 38:12-13)

Verse 14 holds the Key to commanding the Day:

"It takes on form like clay under a seal, And stands out like a garment." (Job 38:14)

Time is a Seal. The Earth is sealed by time. When Time is no more, Day and Night will also cease.

"And the angel which I saw stand upon the sea and upon the earth lifted up his hand to heaven, And sware by him that liveth for ever and ever, who created heaven, and the things that therein are, and the earth, and the things that therein are, and the sea, and the things which are therein, that there should be time no longer: But in the days of the voice of the seventh angel, when he shall begin to sound, the mystery of God should be finished, as he hath declared to his servants the prophets." (Revelation 10:5-7)

The same way the Lord is in Covenant with mankind, He also has a covenant with the Day and the Night:

"And the word of the Lord came unto Jeremiah, saying, Thus saith the Lord; If ye can break my covenant of the day, and my covenant of the night, and that there should not be day and night in their season; Thus saith the Lord; If my covenant be not with day and night, and if I have not appointed the ordinances of heaven and earth..." (Jeremiah 33:19-20, 25)

A good Intercessor, like a good defense attorney, knows the terms of the Covenant or the Law. These are the legalities and technicalities that help us enforce the ordinances of Heaven in the Earth and defeat our wicked opponent Satan.

Let us watch and pray.

Enforce the First Watch of the Night
6pm – 9pm Prayer Watch

Pray for Financial Release

Activate and Deploy the Mantles and the Weapons Reserved For the End-Time Harvest

First Watch of the Night (The Early Night Watch): 6 p.m. to 9 p.m. – This is a critical hour to command the release of financial blessings. In the financial sectors, business sectors and every major system of world currency, the hour of 6 p.m. closes the day and the assessment of the day begins to determine the value of the next trading day. This is a natural and a Spiritual Gate. The new Day does not begin in the morning, but the First Watch of the Night is when you make decrees to shape the New Day.

God has given us His promise to release our Harvest when we release our seed:

"While the earth remaineth, seedtime and harvest, and cold and heat, and summer and winter, and day and night shall not cease." (Genesis 8:22)

We must use this hour to make decrees and pray for the release of the former and the latter rain so that we can enforce the Kingdom of God.

"Be glad then, ye children of Zion, and rejoice in the Lord your God: for he hath given you the former rain moderately, and he will cause to come down for you the rain, the former rain, and the latter rain in the first month." (Joel 2:23)

Every kingdom must have resources in order for the kingdom to prosper, to have longevity and sustainability. What causes Revivals to cease is when there are no resources to sustain the people. This is what released the Miracle of the Fish and Loaves:

"And when it was evening, his disciples came to him, saying, This is a desert place, and the time is now past; send the multitude away, that they may go into the villages, and buy themselves victuals. But Jesus said unto them, They need not depart; give ye them to eat. And they say unto him, We have here but five loaves, and two fishes. He said, Bring them hither to me. And he commanded the multitude to sit down on the grass, and took the five loaves, and the two fishes, and looking up to heaven, he blessed, and brake, and gave the loaves to his disciples, and the disciples to the multitude. And they did all eat, and were filled: and they took up of the fragments that remained twelve baskets full." (Matthew 14:15-20)

The Evening Watch is critical to release provisions that sustain the move of God. This Gate can determine the outcome of the next day and even the next generation. We must be wise.

Scriptures to Meditate on and Things to Pray For:

Release the Wailing Women to Cry Out for the Nation
Study Scriptures: Lamentations 2:18-19

Continued Illumination Throughout the Night Watches

Study Scriptures: Exodus 27:20-21;
                                 Psalm 119:147-148

Pray For Signs, Wonders and Miracles to Be Released

Study Scriptures: 1 Kings 18:29-30; 36-39

Deal With the Destructive Enemy Forces of the Night Watches

Study Scriptures: Isaiah 17:11-14

Pray for the Release of Finances

Study Scriptures: Zechariah 1:17,
                                 Deuteronomy 8:18

Prayer Points

- We activate and deploy the mantles of great revivalists, national deliverers, men and women used by God to do great exploits – let those mantles fall now in the name of Jesus

- We activate and deploy new weapons from the Kingdom of God to confront, dismantle and destroy the trusted weapons of the enemy in the name of Jesus.

- We deactivate satanic activations that were set in motion to disfavor or subvert the Righteous and the Seed of the Righteous in the name of Jesus.

- We decree Divine Judgments against demonic command centers assigned to watch over, monitor and enforce curses and attacks against The Righteous and the seed of The Righteous in Jesus name.

- We speak into the womb of time and release financial revival for our nation and prosperity of the righteous in our nation in the name of Jesus.

- We destroy lack, famine and financial setback and release the economic stability and advancement of our nation, our city, our churches and our families in the name of Jesus.

- We release wisdom and knowledge to overrule greed and ignorance in every system and pillar of our nation in the name of Jesus.

- We command deliverances for those in positions of authority who desire to be responsible and productive in the advancement of the agenda of God for our nation – may they be delivered from the temptations of corruption and theft in the name of Jesus.

- We release divine acceleration in all development of projects – roads, schools, hospitals etc. in the name of Jesus. Let funds earmarked for such development be used for the greatest good of the people in the nation and not to enrich one generation while leaving behind another generation to suffer in the name of Jesus.

- We command empowerment and strength to the middle class in nations that are suffering under the weight of too many rich people not sharing the wealth and too many poor people not receiving relief in the name of Jesus.

- God wants us to be helpers one to another, may our nation receive wisdom for correction and adjustment from God so that we can be delivered from wicked rulers who will take advantage of the oppressive conditions of our nation to keep enriching themselves while punishing the poor and driving the country into economic

ruin – deliver us Oh Lord by the power
of the Blood of Jesus.

- We pray for new millionaires and
  billionaires to rise who will support the
  Kingdom of God and its advancement and
  the release of global revival in the name of
  Jesus.

- We speak into the womb of time and
  legislate by Divine Authority that the
  regulatory systems of our nation will be set
  in place and law enforcement procedures
  will be put in place to prevent prejudices
  and suffering of any one group of people as
  another group executes judgment based on
  gender, ethnicity, tribes or belief systems
  in the name of Jesus.

- Let God's Will for mankind take
  preeminence over wicked legislation and
  overrule technicalities and legalities that
  disfavor and disinherit the minority people
  so that those in the majority rule unjustly
  over them in the name of Jesus.

- Let the wicked lose their position and let
  their seat be overturned now in the name
  of Jesus. Let them lose their position and let

another who will be like Cyrus and favor the cause of righteousness take their place now in the name of Jesus.

- We release the seven-fold Spirit of God to rule over the banking system in our nations and reverse unfavorable interest rates and negotiating conditions on loans that make it difficult for the poor and those in the private sector so that they remain in perpetual debt passed on from generation to generation. Let such systems receive the Fire of God and break their hold over the life of the nation in the name of Jesus.

- We command the unconditional release of the financial prosperity of those in the Kingdom of God. Let money come now in the name of Jesus.

- We decree angelic interventions, angelic undergirding, angelic assistance, angelic reinforcements, and angelic undertakings to be released in this First Watch of the Night to cover us through the Night Watches and beyond in Jesus name.

Confession:

By the power of this confession, I deprogram all satanic programming projected into the womb of my tomorrow in this First Watch of the Night. Through the Blood of Redemption, I command the arrest of all spirits and powers fashioned against me to hinder my advancement through this night and release Glory into tomorrow morning in the name of Jesus. I uproot, tear down and overthrow any seeds that were sown during this day and that are projected to show up tomorrow and hinder my progress, deny my elevation or become a thorn to my peace and a block to my prosperity in the future. I repent for any error in judgment, lack of discernment, or speech that is contrary to God's divine plan to prosper me and do me good and not evil in the land of the living. I release the power to focus and command my mind to be still and receive fresh insight for the Night and tomorrow. I arrest every distraction that attempts to interrupt the heavenly download of instructions and adjustments that need to be made so that I can have good success tomorrow and beyond. Thank you Lord right now in this First Watch of the Night for delivering me through the

Night and into my Glorious future in Jesus name.

Chapter Thirteen

The Second Watch of the Night

Pray for Divine Preparation and Open Doors for the Five-Fold Ministry

The Second Watch of the Night is a Watch of Preparation. God has a plan for you, but the enemy also has a plan for you. Psalm 59 is a prayer of Deliverance against the plan of the enemy that happens at the time of the evening:

"Deliver me from mine enemies, O my God: defend me from them that rise up against me. Deliver me from the workers of iniquity, and save me from bloody men. For, lo, they lie in wait for my soul: the mighty are gathered against me; not for my transgression, nor for my sin, O Lord. They run and prepare themselves without my fault: awake to help me, and behold. Thou therefore, O Lord God of hosts, the God of Israel, awake to visit all the heathen: be not merciful to any wicked transgressors. Selah." (Psalm 59:1-5)

Here the battle strategy of the enemy is being described. The Psalmist describes them using a set time to "run and prepare themselves".

What we cannot expect is that we can ask God to be awake to our cause, if we are not awake, on our Watch and lifting up prayer. If we think we are not in a battle because we didn't start the fight, Beloved, the battle wages against you and while God is your Defender, your best Offense is preparation by prayer. God responds to our prayers. He wants us to be prepared and this is the Watch for Divine Preparation to deal with the Voice of the Enemy. Psalm 59 goes on to describe what the enemy does in the evening watches:

"They return at evening: they make a noise like a dog, and go round about the city. Behold, they belch out with their mouth: swords are in their lips: for who, say they, doth hear?" (Psalm 59:6-7)

The plan of the enemy is to destroy and uproot all the work that was done during the day. To discredit God and overturn the victories that were fought and won by the righteous. This is why we can never stop praying. We are only as victorious as our last victory. We must continue to fight the good fight of faith until the end. The enemy counts on you not speaking up when he is speaking against you.

His strength is our ignorance of his devices.
The psalmist instructs us to pray:

"But thou, O Lord, shalt laugh at them; thou shalt have all the heathen in derision. Because of his strength will I wait upon thee: for God is my defense. The God of my mercy shall prevent me: God shall let me see my desire upon mine enemies. Slay them not, lest my people forget: scatter them by thy power; and bring them down, O Lord our shield. For the sin of their mouth and the words of their lips let them even be taken in their pride: and for cursing and lying which they speak. Consume them in wrath, consume them, that they may not be: and let them know that God ruleth in Jacob unto the ends of the earth. Selah." (Psalm 59:8-13)

Here the Psalmist says, don't take the enemy out – but let us use this time for preparation and target practice to defeat the enemy and cause them to scatter. God uses some enemies to prepare us for greater warfare. To show us battle strategies so that we can gain an advantage over our enemy and understand the weapons of our warfare. The psalmist shows us that this exercise is to prepare us for future battles:

"And at evening let them return; and let them make a noise like a dog, and go round about the city. Let them wander up and down for meat, and grudge if they be not satisfied." (Psalm 59:14-15)

Pray for the Church of Christ to Preach, Teach, Prophesy, Evangelize, Cast Out Demons, Raise Up Prayer Warriors and Intercessors

This is why during this time the Church of Christ must be ready to preach, teach, prophesy, evangelize, cast out demons and raise up prayer warriors and intercessors. We must not sit back on our past victories reminiscing about days gone by. We must pray for a fresh wind of Revival and practice the foundations of our faith that enforce the Kingdom of God. The enemy will keep coming and so we must be vigilant to maintain our position of advantage.

The Scriptures say the same enemy returns again evening after evening, making the same noises, telling the same lies, looking for the prey they released a sword against the night before. He came in verse 6 to release the sword of his mouth and to release his plan of destruction. Now we see in verse 14 he returns to look for the "meat". He is looking to see what was destroyed the night before. This is Satan's plan. But, our preparation will always produce his solemn defeat. The Psalmist declares:

"But I will sing of thy power; yea, I will sing aloud of thy mercy in the morning: for thou hast been my defense and refuge in the day of my trouble. Unto thee, O my strength, will I sing: for God is my defense, and the God of my mercy." (Psalm 59:16-17)

Beloved, you must take hold of the Night Watches if you are going to sing in the morning and be delivered in the Day of Trouble. God is our defense and prayer is our offense. In order to rule in the midst of our enemies, we must know how to deploy the key of prayer and Divine Preparation. Preparation is the key to release Goodness and Mercy to follow us:

"Thou preparest a table before me in the presence of mine enemies: thou anointest my head with oil; my cup runneth over. Surely goodness and mercy shall follow me all the days of my life: and I will dwell in the house of the Lord for ever." (Psalm 23:5-6)

Let us watch and pray.

Enforce the Second Watch of the Night
9pm – Midnight

The Second Watch of the Night (The Late Night Watch) 9pm to Midnight – is a time for thanksgiving; time for visitation; the time when the Lord prepares you to receive many acts of change in the earth. You must be prepared before the Midnight Watch. It is a time for the transfer of wealth as in Exodus 12:31, 35-36 which says Pharaoh called for Moses and Aaron and released them and they responded by executing what the Lord had already promised them He would do:

"And he called for Moses and Aaron by night, and said, Rise up, and get you forth from among my people, both ye and the children of Israel; and go, serve the Lord, as ye have said. And the children of Israel did according to the word of Moses; and they borrowed of the Egyptians jewels of silver, and jewels of gold, and raiment: And the Lord gave the people favour in the sight of the Egyptians, so that they lent unto them such things as they required. And they spoiled the Egyptians."

We need wealth to transfer from the Kingdom of Darkness in order to build and establish the Kingdom of God. This is the hour to enforce the transfer of a nation's wealth to another nation. The Watch Hour to command cancellation of National Debt and to enforce Economic Revival.

Midnight is symbolic of intense darkness, but God is the light in the darkness and releases strategy during this time of preparation in order for us to overcome the strategies of the enemy during the Midnight Watch.

The Second Watch of the Night comes when we get scattered. We leave our places of business, fellowship, even the center of family life. The parents are alone in their rooms and the children are alone in their rooms. This is the time where your child may be in their bedroom, but in light of this being the Age of New Media, there is the potential for them to be located in another continent through a social media connection. We must watch and pray. Develop a habit of discipline during this hour that ensures we do not lose the next generation but that rather we learn to get the greatest good out of this Age of New Media.

Scriptures to Meditate on and Things to Pray For:

Release the Transfer of Wealth Over Nations
Study Scriptures: Isaiah 23:17-18; Isaiah 60:5 & 11; Isaiah 61:6; Isaiah 66:12

Release the Transfer of Wealth for the Righteous and the Seed of the Righteous
Study Scriptures: Proverbs 13:22; Ecclesiastes 2:26, Proverbs 10:22; Psalm 39:6; Psalm 112:1-3; Job 27:13-17

Pray For Obedience to Fulfill the Laws of the Kingdom and Receive the Rewards
Study Scriptures: Psalm 37:21; Job 22:21-26; Psalm 111:1-10; Proverbs 22:22-23

Release the Financial Inheritance of the Righteous and the Seed of the Righteous
Study Scriptures: Joshua 24:13; Proverbs 13:22, Ecclesiastes 2:26; Zechariah 14:14

Prayer Points

- We pray for the recovery of currency in our nation and the alleviation of National Debt

and for favorable terms and settlements
of all National Debts and related issues in
the Global Markets in the name of Jesus.

- Let there be economic revival and financial
recovery now in the name of Jesus.

- We arrest and break the curse of financial
drought and famine over our nation, our
churches, our family and the work of our
hands in Jesus name.
- We revoke the curse of spiritual drought
and famine over our nation, our city, our
churches and our family in the name of
Jesus.

- We command the release of wealth and
riches for the End-Time Harvest in the
name of Jesus.

- We break embargoes and dismantle
whatever is holding back the financial
channels of The Righteous in the name of
Jesus.

- We release the financial channels, financial
helpers, prosperity and Grace for growth in
The Church and over The Righteous in the
name of Jesus.

- We decree many streams of income, multiplicity of blessings, favor, opportunities, new enterprise, raises, increase and innovations for The Righteous and The Seed of Righteous   in the name of Jesus.

- We decree Divine Fulfillment for The Righteous as the Mantles and Weapons of Warfare are deployed to advance the Kingdom of God in this generation and the next generation in the name of Jesus.

- We command the visitation of angels, the release of miracles and supernatural signs and wonders to be a regular occurrence in our churches and wherever the men and women gather to pray in the name of Jesus.

- We call for Divine Manifestations to be evident and supernatural occurrences to be documented in this generation to give hope to the next generation in Jesus name.

- We interrupt any satanic carrier of satanic pregnancies, conceptions and agendas and terminate their assignment and the carriers of the assignment.

- We interrupt satanic vehicles deployed to kill, to steal and destroy the righteous in the name of Jesus.

- We interrupt and cancel the assignment of men and women who have sold themselves, their conscious, their bodies, their souls and their spirits to Satan to do evil against the children of God and terminate them in the name of Jesus. Let them receive Fire now in the name of Jesus.

- We command the release of Revivalists, Community Transformers, Prophets, Apostles and all who have been captured and bound by legions - We command them loosed and set free from demonic forces in the name of Jesus.

- We interrupt and arrest every demon of addictions deployed to destroy the lives of Revivalists, Community Transformers, Prophets, Apostles and great intercessors – every drug addiction, nicotine addiction, alcohol addiction, and pornographic addiction be arrested in the name of Jesus.

- We call for Divine Judgment against the demon working through the internet, the media, political and social institutions of this age – We block them and shut them down – We execute the judgment written in Isaiah 49:24-26 in the name of Jesus.

Confession:

By Divine authority, I deploy the Voice of the Blood of Jesus to silence every contrary voice that blocks my ability to tune into the frequency of Heaven. Silence the voice of guilt, shame and accusation that keeps me from receiving fresh insight and revelation from the throne room of Jehovah in the name of Jesus. By Divine Authority and through the Blood of Jesus I command my immediate and unconditional release from the captivity of wicked taskmasters and the web of indebtedness that keeps me from giving into the Kingdom of God. By obedience and the key of sacrifice I open my channels of financial access and release all the blessings God has appointed for me in this season. I block all satanic agents policing my breakthrough and command their arrest now in the name of Jesus. I will not be a victim and my children will not be victimized in the name of Jesus. Release the keys of knowledge and wisdom for my specific financial situation and help me walk in obedience to fulfill your instructions so that this will be my year to walk in true financial freedom in the name of Jesus.

Chapter Fourteen

The Third Watch of the Night

The Warfare Watch – The Watch of Deliverance

This is the Watch of the Warrior. The Bible says in Isaiah 9:5-7:

"For every battle of the warrior is with confused noise, and garments rolled in blood; but this shall be with burning and fuel of fire. For unto us a child is born, unto us a son is given: and the government shall be upon his shoulder: and his name shall be called Wonderful, Counsellor, The mighty God, The everlasting Father, The Prince of Peace. Of the increase of his government and peace there shall be no end, upon the throne of David, and upon his kingdom, to order it, and to establish it with judgment and with justice from henceforth even for ever. The zeal of the Lord of hosts will perform this."

The Battle of the Warrior is what precedes the establishment of God's government – the Kingdom. The Battle is ongoing until the full establishment of God's promises. This is the Watch Hour to release the Zeal of the Lord.

The Zeal of the Lord releases the angelic activity that happens at the Midnight Watch to enforce the ordinances of God. The Bible says many things about the activity of Angels and of Mighty Men and Women that happened in the Midnight Watch.

When Pharaoh would not let the people go in Exodus 12:29, God released an Angel to execute the written judgment of Exodus 11:4:

"And it came to pass, that at midnight the Lord smote all the firstborn in the land of Egypt, from the firstborn of Pharaoh that sat on his throne unto the firstborn of the captive that was in the dungeon; and all the firstborn of cattle."

When the enemy set a trap for Samson, God gave him the Gates of the city at Midnight in Judges 16:2-3:

"And it was told the Gazites, saying, Samson is come hither. And they compassed him in, and laid wait for him all night in the gate of the city, and were quiet all the night, saying, In the morning, when it is day, we shall kill him. And Samson lay till midnight, and arose at midnight, and took the doors of the gate of the city, and the two posts, and went away with them, bar

and all, and put them upon his shoulders, and carried them up to the top of an hill that is before Hebron."

This is a time for the single to be located by the Door of Marriage. The Bible says in Ruth 3:7-9 that Boaz became aware that he was the Kinsman Redeemer at Midnight:

"And when Boaz had eaten and drunk, and his heart was merry, he went to lie down at the end of the heap of corn: and she came softly, and uncovered his feet, and laid her down. And it came to pass at midnight, that the man was afraid, and turned himself: and, behold, a woman lay at his feet. And he said, Who art thou? And she answered, I am Ruth thine handmaid: spread therefore thy skirt over thine handmaid; for thou art a near kinsman."

The enemy has a plan to destroy us at Midnight. If we slumber and are unaware, he will execute demonic transfers and wicked switches in the Midnight Watch. He comes to steal, kill and to destroy the Divine Destiny of the Righteous at Midnight. The Bible says in 1 Kings 3:19-21:

"And this woman's child died in the night; because she overlaid it. And she arose at midnight, and took my son from beside me, while thine handmaid slept, and laid it in her bosom, and laid her dead child in my bosom. And when I rose in the morning to give my child suck, behold, it was dead: but when I had considered it in the morning, behold, it was not my son, which I did bear."

Job 34:20 says premature death happens suddenly at Midnight:

"In a moment shall they die, and the people shall be troubled at midnight, and pass away: and the mighty shall be taken away without hand."

In the Midnight Watch, God will bring your deliverance, but you will need to get up and be on your Watch.

"At midnight I will arise to give thanks unto thee because of thy righteous judgments." (Psalm 119:62)

Midnight is the Hour of the Bridegroom. The Bible tells us in Matthew 25:1-13 that the Kingdom of God can come suddenly to deliver those who are ready, who have the Oil of Anointing and who are awake at Midnight:

"Then shall the kingdom of heaven be likened unto ten virgins, which took their lamps, and went forth to meet the bridegroom. And five of them were wise, and five were foolish. They that were foolish took their lamps, and took no oil with them: But the wise took oil in their vessels with their lamps. While the bridegroom tarried, they all slumbered and slept."

This is the condition of the church today. If we don't get up and pray we will just be waiting for the Lord to return and we may find ourselves asleep when He comes.

And at midnight there was a cry made, Behold, the bridegroom cometh; go ye out to meet him. Then all those virgins arose, and trimmed their lamps.

There is a cry being made today to "Get up! Get on your Watch. It's time to pray!" If we are going to see our nation, our churches and our families delivered, we are going to have to pray for illumination, for strategy and we can never let the Light of Revelatory prayers grow dim:

And the foolish said unto the wise, Give us of your oil; for our lamps are gone out. But the wise answered, saying, Not so; lest there be not enough for us and you: but go ye rather to them that sell, and buy for yourselves. And while they went to buy, the bridegroom came; and they that were ready went in with him to the marriage: and the door was shut.

There are Gates and there are Doors in every Watch. The Gates can be possessed. The Doors can be entered. It is the Time that must be discerned or we will miss our opportunity to possess our possessions and enter the doors of blessing:

Afterward came also the other virgins, saying, Lord, Lord, open to us. But he answered and said, Verily I say unto you, I know you not. Watch therefore, for ye know neither the day nor the hour wherein the Son of man cometh."

You can miss your moment of breakthrough, release and blessing. You can find yourself outside when you should be on the other side. It is up to you to decide to hear the cry in this generation and arise to your role as an Intercessor. Let us watch and pray!

Enforce the Third Watch of the Night
Midnight to 3 a.m.

The Third Watch of the Night (The Warfare Watch) Midnight to 3 a.m. – is a time for prayers of protection and strength to overcome; time for outpouring of the spirit of grace; to overcome every limitation of gifts and anointing; special time for divine governments; overruling human decrees to give an angelic release. The Third Watch of the Night is one of the most important watches. It is the time in which spiritual warfare takes place and where satanic activities are at its height. It is during this watch that Satan and the various troops of the infernal kingdom operate the most because their weapon is darkness and they take advantage when we are asleep to sow tares and wreak havoc on any pending harvest.

It is a time to pray against all sexual immorality such as fornication, adultery, prostitution, orgies, occult sexual activities, homosexuality, sexual abuse and rape. This is the time to awake out of sleep and confront every storm, distraction and spirits of Diablos and Apollyon that are programmed to bring sudden destruction, loss and devastation. This is the time to enforce that your victory over spirits of fear and terror.

It is during this watch that the Angel of Death goes through communities, cities, nations and the world to bring death and destruction to the disobedient and the enemy also sends the spirit of premature death to snatch life suddenly.

It is time for dreams and visions and it is also time for miracles to be performed as well as covenants to be remembered.

Scriptures to Meditate on and Things to Pray For:

Pray for the Release of Angelic Assistance Against Satanic Plots
Study Scriptures: Genesis 28:10-19; Judges 16:2-3; Acts 23:19-31,; Acts 27:25-44; 2 Kings 19:32-35; Acts 16:25-34

Release Believers From Demonic Strongholds & Prisons
Study Scriptures: Acts 16:25-34; Psalm 119:61-62; 1 Corinthians

10:13; 2 Corinthians 10:3-4; Judges 6 Isaiah 23:11

Enlighten The Eyes of Intercessors Set Over Nations

Study Scriptures: 1 Thessalonians 5:23; Proverbs 20:27; Psalms 13:3, Psalms 18:28-32; Job 32:8, Matthew 13:25; Mark 1:35; Ephesians 1:18; 2 Corinthians 4:4

Pray for Marriages

Study Scriptures: Matthew 25:6 -10; Ruth 3:7-11; Isaiah 34:16

Pray for Leaders and The Peace of Nations

Study Scriptures: 2 Kings 19:32-35; 1 Timothy 2:1-4; Romans 13:1; 2 Chronicles 7:14; Jeremiah 29:7; 1 Peter 2:17; Daniel 2:20-23; Proverbs 21:1; Psalms 22:27-28; Job 12:23-25; Psalm 2:1-4; Titus 3:1-2; Daniel 9:18-19; Matthew 12:25; Proverbs 28:2; Leviticus 26:6

Pray for the Conviction of Sin and Immorality

Study Scriptures: John 16:8; Isaiah 6:5; Acts

16:29; Ezra 10:1; Psalm 51; Psalm 38:18; Hosea 6:1; Jonah 3:6-9

Pray Against Sexual Sins of Homosexuality and Rape

Study Scriptures: Romans 1:21-32; Read Judges Chapters 19-21, Pray against the perversion of this generation

Pray for the Preparation of the Church

Study Scriptures: Matthew 25:1-13; Revelation 19:7-9; Revelation 21:2-9; John 3:29; Ephesians 5:27

Pray Against Premature Death in the House of the Righteous

Study Scriptures: Exodus 12-14; Job 27:20; Job 34:25; Job 36:20; Job 34:20

Prayer Points

- We command deliverance and the unconditional release of all those held bound by strife, conflict and disharmony in our nation, in our communities, in our churches and the families of The Righteous in Jesus name.

- We curse the seed of strife, conflict, disharmony, confusion and misrepresentation that is causing unrest in nations, communities, churches and families in the name of Jesus.

- Let the spirit of terror and fear seducing nations, communities, churches and families be arrested now in the name of Jesus.

- We deploy the Blood of Jesus to overrule satanic predictions, witchcraft manipulations and demonic lies released by the enemy to cause destruction and confusion in nations, communities, churches and families of the Righteous in the name of Jesus.

- We arrest all demonic harassments and vexation against the seed of The Righteous in the name of Jesus

- We interrupt messengers of Satan assigned to buffet The Church and restrict The Five-Fold Ministry in this generation and to limit the move of God for the next generation. Let it be interrupted and arrested now in the name of Jesus.

- We block demonic openings in The Church and in the life of The Righteous and the Seed of the Righteous in the name of Jesus. Let the Righteous be alert, aware and receive Divine Illumination now in the name of Jesus.

- We disadvantage every advantage of the enemy and strip the enemy of his trusted weapons against the righteous and The Church in the name of Jesus.

- We interrupt and overturn any evil agenda on satanic calendars against the righteous in strategic gate or door of opportunity in the name of Jesus. Let every satanic programming within the womb of time be overturned and overwritten by the Supreme Sacrifice of the Blood of Jesus.

- We interrupt and override the weapons deployed against The Church in the Heavens, in the Earth, in the Forest Kingdom, in the Animal Kingdom and in the Water Kingdom in Jesus name.

- We override and interrupt any beast and disembodied spirit who deploys strange winds, rough winds, creates turbulence, storms, earthquakes, tsunamis, floods, strange weather, hurricanes or any other crises using the elements against the Body of Christ, The Church and The Five-Fold Ministry in the name of Jesus.

- We interrupt that which has been deployed to hurt The Church in this Night Watch and we decree and declare the opposite of demonic predictions shall occur according to Esther 9:1.

- We declare counter predictions against their predictions and counter commands against their commands and release blessings, honor and glory into the future of our nation, our communities, our churches and our families in the name of Jesus.

- We command the freedom and unconditional release of the captives in the name of Jesus. Let chains break and the prison doors restricting the Righteous and the Seed of the Righteous be opened now in the name of Jesus.

- We cancel every surprise that is projected against the Righteous and the Seed of the Righteous and that has been sent from the witchcraft and the marine kingdoms. Let it be overturned now in the name of Jesus.

- We arrest that which is on assignment to kill, to steal and to destroy the Body of Christ and The Generals within The Body by the Supreme Sacrifice of the Blood of Jesus

- We command the deliverance of potential future leaders of The Body of Christ being held at ransom by the enemy. We command their deliverance now in the name of Jesus.

- We release the Blood of Jesus and the Spirit of the living God to invade Religious Institutions in our nation so that people would once again turn to God for solutions.

- Let our nation enter a time of national repentance so that God can release healing for our nation in the name of Jesus.

- We pray that the church would once again make a positive impact on the nation and we overturn religious conflicts and unrest seeking to destroy national peace and fellowship among the citizens of the nation in the name of Jesus.

- We release Godly marriages and divine connections that have the potential to build the Kingdom and release Godly offspring to enforce the plans of God in the next generation. We pray for the release of those marriages and secure the fruit of the womb through the Blood of Jesus.

Confession:

May the wicked be driven away like the wind. Uncovered like darkness when Light shines in secret places. May every plot, scheme, plan and time-sensitive tactic of the enemy be overthrown in the Name of Jesus. May the righteous run for cover and be found by You. May every plan of the enemy to overthrow my assignment be located and dealt with thoroughly by the Hand and the Sword of Jehovah. May every evil, sinful, self-serving work of my hands be judged and purged by the fire of true repentance. Not from a place of deep sorrow alone, but from a place of revelatory understanding. May these next days, weeks, months show me for sure that my Redeemer lives. Where traps and snares have been laid, may they burn like dry thickets and the leaves of late fall at the burning of the Lord's rebuke. Father, deliver me from the snare of the fowler and the desire of the wicked one. Locate me, find me wherever I am lost - seek and save me for Your Eternal Purpose. Deliver me from any spirit of self-destruction and restore my Hope. You are my Eternal Hope. Lord, help me. Help me in secret places; in places where I have no voice and no representatives. Where there is no one to speak for me, may the Lord be my attorney. May my advocate represent me where I have no defense. May the Blood of Jesus be my defense and my Strong Tower of safety. Where I have missed the mark, and my life is out of Divine Alignment with your purpose - save me Lord! Realign my purpose and change my course in the Night Watches so that when the breaking of Day comes, I will see the salvation of the Lord! In spite of my enemies and every ill will for my public humiliation, I invoke the Word written in Jeremiah 20:10-11:

"For I heard the defaming of many, fear on every side. Report, say they, and we will report it. All my familiars watched for my halting,

saying, Peradventure he will be enticed, and we shall prevail against him, and we shall take our revenge on him. But the Lord is with me as a mighty terrible one: therefore my persecutors shall stumble, and they shall not prevail: they shall be greatly ashamed; for they shall not prosper: their everlasting confusion shall never be forgotten."

Chapter Fifteen

The Fourth Watch of the Night

Pray for the Release of Spiritual and Natural Blessings

This is the time to command the morning and to program the will of God for your life into the new day. The morning has a womb and it is the seed that we plant into our morning that produces fruit for us to harvest throughout the day. This Watch is called "The Morning Watch" because it is the Exit Gate of the Night and the Entrance of a New Day.

It is during the morning that we get our instructions and directions on how we are to move throughout our day. We are essentially like soldiers waiting for our Commander and Chief to give us our battle strategies. How are we to know the traps that the enemy has set for us if we do not consult with God first? Before we make any moves in our day, we must first go to God in prayer early in the morning before the dawn breaks to get our orders for the day.

This Hour is a critical time to enforce the victory of the Warfare that was revealed in the

Midnight Watch. This is the hour when God will give us new strength, angelic reinforcements and fresh insight to completely overthrow our strong enemy.

In 1 Samuel chapter 11, after Saul had been anointed by Samuel to be the King over Israel, Nahash the Ammonite set up camp to fight the people of Jabesh Gilead and to take them captive along with their resources and land. The Elders of Jabesh Gilead asked Nahash to make treaty with them so that they would not be overtaken. Nahash would only agree to make treaty if all their right eyes could be gouged out.

The enemy is never a good business partner. We cannot make deals with the devil and expect that he will be fair and equitable. We must treat him as Jesus did and enforce his sound defeat. He will return again and again, and God will continue to give us the victory if we maintain our position and resist his tactics. Look at how Saul handled Nahash.

The men of Jabesh asked for grace for seven days to send messengers throughout Israel to see if any would come and rescue them. The messengers went to Gibeah and reported the terms to the people.

When Saul heard the words, *the Spirit of the Lord fell on him*. Saul divided the people into three companies. The three groups entered the camp of the Ammonites during the **morning watch** (the Fourth Watch of the Night) and kept attacking until the **heat of the day** (the Third Watch of the Day), until those who remained were so scattered that no two of them were left together.

This is the Hour to scatter the enemy. This is the Watch that those involved in witchcraft, the occult, new age, and satanic worship usually perform their activities through astral projection and are returning back to their bases or bodies. They understand that their trusted weapons have a limitation. They understand that when the daybreaks, they can no more operate under the cloak of darkness. The Bible says in Ecclesiastes 12:3-7:

"In the day when the keepers of the house shall tremble, and the strong men shall bow themselves, and the grinders cease because they are few, and those that look out of the windows be darkened, And the doors shall be shut in the

streets, when the sound of the grinding is low, and he shall rise up at the voice of the bird, and all the daughters of musick shall be brought low; Also when they shall be afraid of that which is high, and fears shall be in the way, and the almond tree shall flourish, and the grasshopper shall be a burden, and desire shall fail: because man goeth to his long home, and the mourners go about the streets: Or ever the silver cord be loosed, or the golden bowl be broken, or the pitcher be broken at the fountain, or the wheel broken at the cistern. Then shall the dust return to the earth as it was: and the spirit shall return unto God who gave it."

But, Job 38:12-13 says that when we command our morning – we can shake the wicked out of our day:

"Hast thou commanded the morning since thy days; and caused the dayspring to know his place; That it might take hold of the ends of the earth, that the wicked might be shaken out of it?"

Command Money, Wealth, Fortunes, Power and Influence To Change Hands

The Morning Watch is the Fourth Watch of the Night. This watch is the Gate of Exit for the Night and Entrance of a new day. The morning watch begins at 3:00 a.m. and ends at 6:00 a.m. This watch is linked with the approaching of the morning light and the breaking of dawn. When we are on this Watch, we can see the plans of the enemy and discern the strategies of God.

There is a proverb that "Your current condition in life is a result of your past position in prayer". This is the Hour where the outcome of whatever you must face during the day can be established in the womb of intercession. When we seek advanced knowledge from the Lord, He will not only show us the plan of the enemy, just as he did for Saul against the Ammonites, he will show us exactly what to do and give us the total victory.

Matthew 24:43 says: *"But know this, that if the goodman of the house had known in what watch the thief would come, he would have watched, and would not have suffered his house to be broken up."*

The Lord said if we would arise when He called us, then we would hear and see during the night so we could rule during the day. If you are going to rule in the midst of your enemies, you will need the key of Revelation. You will need advanced knowledge to take out the strongholds of your enemy.

"Men do not despise a thief, if he steal to satisfy his soul when he is hungry; But if he be found, he shall restore sevenfold; he shall give all the substance of his house." Proverbs 6:30-31

John 10:10 says the thief comes to "steal, kill and destroy." When we are on this Watch, it is our time to not only catch the thief, but to command restoration of stolen goods, lost opportunities, diverted blessings and anything that we are missing that we should have. Beloved, we are not only asking for restoration, but we must demand that he pay us back with seven-fold interest. We are not ignorant of his devices and we refuse to perish. This is a strategic watch to command the release of Spiritual and natural blessings.

Let us watch and pray.

The Fourth Watch of the Night (The Morning Watch) 3 a.m. to 6 a.m. – Time to pray for freedom of the Church. Pray for angelic activity or intervention; the time when God releases the dew of heaven; time for blessings from heaven above; blessings of the deep that lies beneath; blessings of the womb; blessings of our fathers and ancestors to be released. This Watch is a time to enforce Divine Restoration and recovery of stolen goods.

This is a time to release one of the greatest spiritual blessings in the church today – supernatural healing. The ministry of Christ is mark by the Gift of Healing and the casting out of demons. This power comes by prayer and is sustained by prayer. The Bible says:

"And at even, when the sun did set, they brought unto him all that were diseased, and them that were possessed with devils. And all the city was gathered together at the door. And he healed many that were sick of divers diseases, and cast out many devils; and suffered not the devils to speak, because they knew him. And in the morning, rising up a great while before day, he

went out, and departed into a solitary place, and there prayed. And Simon and they that were with him followed after him. And when they had found him, they said unto him, All men seek for thee." (Mark 1:32-37)

The Church must heal the sick and cast out demons. Jesus started the healing revival at Sunset, but early the next morning before day, He went to a solitary place to pray. If we are going to experience Revival, we must be committed not just to pray once, but to keep on praying so that we can receive power, fresh fire and angelic assistance from on high.

Scriptures to Meditate on and Things to Pray For:

Pray for the Release of Healing Power and Salvation in the Church
Study Scriptures: Isaiah 58:8; Isaiah 62:1-12

Pray for Illumination to Avert and Destroy the Plan of Darkness
Study Scriptures: Psalm 18:28; Job 3:5-9; James 1:17

Pray for Miracles, Signs and Wonders
Study Scriptures: Mark 1:32-37; Mark 6:45-51; Revelation 8:3-5

Pray for The Release of Divine Judgment of God Against the Wicked

Study Scriptures: Job 38:12-13; Ecclesiastes 12:6, Isaiah 17:14; Genesis 19:15

Pray for Revival and Fresh Strength to Come to the Body of Christ

Study Scriptures: Matthew 28:1-3; Isaiah 60:1-; Psalms 110:3; Genesis 45:25-28; Judges 15:18-19; 1 Kings 17:22; Psalms 85:6; Psalms 138:7; Isaiah 64:1

Pray for the Release of Blessings for the Righteous

Study Scriptures: Genesis 32:24-26; Prov. 6:30-31

Pray for Battle Strategies for the Day

Study Scriptures: 1 Samuel 11:6-11; Exodus 14:23-25; Job 38:12; Proverbs 8:17; Luke 1:78-79

Prayer Points

- In the name of Jesus we release the Sword of Jehovah to break the silver cord of spirits without bodies and to crush the golden bowl of those who monitor and police the life and destiny of the righteous.

- We command the dayspring to appear suddenly and shake the wicked out of their position of advantage in the name of Jesus.

- We enforce the judgment written in Isaiah 17:14 and command every thief of our good fortunes in our nation, in our communities, our churches and our families – we command their arrest now in the name of Jesus.

- We arrest the thief and overthrow the robber in the name of Jesus. Let the wickedness of the wicked come to an end.

- We enforce the judgment written over those who have taken the nation hostage according to the word written in Gen. 19:15 and Jeremiah 19. Let the devices of the crafty be dismantled and overthrown now in the name of Jesus.

- We execute the judgment written and overturn satanic cartels and arrest all those who operate in the occult to control the gates of nations, communities and families in the name of Jesus.

- We command dormant gifts of the Righteous and the Seed of the Righteous to rise, shine and resurrect in the name of Jesus. Let wells of anointing of power break and left the gifts be used to edify the church and advance the Kingdom of God in this generation and the next generation in the name of Jesus.

- We call on the Angel of the Lord to release earthquakes, thunders, and lightening to roll away spiritual and natural stones of embargoes and restrictions that are covering the Glory of the Righteous and the Seed of the Righteous in the name of Jesus. Let the stones be rolled away now!

- We command Divine Illumination for discernment, wisdom and understanding of the enemies of this age, the tactics of their warfare and the power of their weapons so that we can disarm, dismantle and destroy all the works of darkness in the name of Jesus.

- Thy Kingdom Come this day in Power, in Glory, in Manifestations of Signs, Wonders, Miracles, Healings, the casting out of demons, the downfall of wicked systems and the overthrow of evil rulers – we deploy the Zeal of the Lord into our Day to superimpose the plan of God over all the plans of the enemy.

- Let God arise and all his enemies be scattered today in the name of Jesus!

Confession

Help me Lord! Deliver me Lord! Send me help from the sanctuary. Deliverance is the bread of your children. I am your child, may I see deliverance in the days to come. Lord, Thy Will be done. Thy Kingdom purpose for my life - please let Thy Kingdom Come. My greatest benefit to your house is to fulfill my heavenly purpose. The purpose for which I was born and permitted to break into earth's atmosphere and that for which I still have breath and life. I want what You want. Confirm me, shape me, mold me! Deliver me for Your Namesake. Help me never to grieve the Holy Spirit. I want the Holy Spirit to remain with me always. Help me to be more sensitive, alert and alive in the Spirit. Help me find my place in the Earth. Place me, plant me, establish me and help me find the place where I will be of the most use in the nation, the community, and the family of God. I will be effective for the Kingdom of God. I am thankful for every gift You have given me. Help me use them wisely and help me finish the Work for which You have given me these gifts. I need finishing Grace. Thank You for helping me Lord.

Chapter Sixteen

Release Prophetic Intercessors

Prayer Points to Release the Voice of
Intercession to Guide Nations

- We deploy the judgment written in Numbers 23:23 and break every spirit of divination and enchantment that has captured, grounded and resisted the voice of prophecy and the spirit of intercession that God uses to guide nations – let that power and bewitchment break now in the name of Jesus!

- We command the veil that covers all nations and blocks the Spirit of Intercession and the cry of the lamentation of nations – let that veil catch Fire now in the name of Jesus!

- We deploy the efficacy of the Blood of Jesus to invade satanic strongholds, witchcraft covens and demonic record books that monitor the progress and movements of the Righteous in order to enforce generational curses and spiritual setback for those who are marked to deliver nations, communities, and families in the name of Jesus.

- We command their unconditional release now in the name of Jesus. We send Fire and Angelic power to unseat the strongman, break the chains and remove all restrictions over the Intercessors of this generation. Let them go free now in the name of Jesus!

- We release the Voice of the Blood to overrule handwriting and ordinances that are contrary and being used to raise an objection to the release of every Intercessor and Prayer Warrior who must be released now in this age and dispensation to ensure the advancement of the Kingdom of God. Let the Voice of the Blood overrule every objection of the enemy and let them be released unconditionally from wherever they are bound in the name of Jesus.

- We release the Spirit of Prophecy that reveals Christ to nations, to communities, to families, to the lost, to the unsaved, to the confused, to the broken, to the hurting, to all those who have been bound by the cares of this world and the conditions of their birth and who the enemy is using these circumstances to destroy nations and to cause wars – let the Spirit of Prophecy be released now to bring reconciliation, hope and the love of God, ourselves and our fellow man in the name of Jesus!

- Let the Spirit of Intercession overshadow the church and produce conviction, repentance and the change that comes from times of refreshing in the Lord. Let the Revival that is produced by true repentance come over our nations, our communities, our churches and our families in the name of Jesus.

- By the power of the Blood of Jesus, we break and renounce every covenant with any satanic altar or deity that was entered into by our ancestors and enforce and solidify a national covenant with the Lord Jesus Christ through the confession of salvation and the power of the efficacy of the Cross of the Lord Jesus Christ.

- We break the power of Satanic covenants being used to govern nations, to manipulate elections, to use the media and the marketplace to enforce satanic agendas and control national currencies through wicked leadership – let that power receive Fire now and let the covenant be broken in the name of Jesus.

Pray for the Heavens to Open and A Fresh Move of the Holy Spirit

- Release the Spirit of Revival to bring a refreshing spiritual revival, economic revival, a love revolution in nations that destroys and dismantles the spirit of hate, terror and fear of one another that is destroying nations. Let Revival Fire come and Revival Waters flow. Revive us Oh Lord! Send a refreshing that reminds the Nations you are enthroned round about them in the name of Jesus!

- Now Lord let every other covenant, altar, demonic stronghold or satanic relationship that is being enforced by wicked strong men, persons without bodies or spiritual wickedness be confronted through the Blood of Jesus Christ and let their power be broken off our nations, our communities, our families and the Intercessors and the Deliverers of this generation and the next generation now in the name of Jesus!

- We will fast and pray and cry out for Angelic reinforcement to unseat princes that sit over nations to deploy wicked rulership and ground the progress, advancement and prosperity of the nation and its people. We disallow it and lift up a resistance in prayer to break the resistance of principalities, thrones and dominions that are unauthorized when we are willing to exercise our Dominion Mandate. We unseat them now and command them to lose their hold, cease their operation and give up their power now in the name of Jesus. Let the nations come to order and the Will of God be enforced over the nation, its leadership and its citizens in the name of Jesus.

- We will not serve mammon, any spiritual husband/wife, demonic altar that calls for money or blood or any other sacrifice and we soak ourselves in the Blood of Jesus through prayer and intercession and effectively rescind, overturn and destroy any object or wicked gadget, device, handwritings the enemy is using according to Colossians 2:14 – let the Fire of God, burn and destroy the handwritings now!

Let the Lord make an open show of those who oppress nations and subvert the Will of God to keep the people in bondage.

- From the throne room perspective we shut down every door of demonic access and open the door of Hope for ourselves, our children, our spouses, our church and our nation to escape and we command our immediate, unconditional release through the Blood of Jesus!

Epilogue

Famous Prayer Watches That Produced National Revival

"But the end of all things is at hand: be ye therefore sober, and watch unto prayer." (1 Peter 4:7)

1. Bangor, Ireland 555 A.D.

In a little village in Northern Ireland 2,000-3,000 people began praying 24 hours a day with particular emphasis on the night watches. This continued for several hundred years and became a center of revival as the fall of the Roman Empire hit and the Dark Ages took over Europe during the 6th-9th century AD.

2. The Island of Rhodes, 1080 A.D.

A Christian order, the Knights of Saint John Watch established 24-hour prayer to *"Stand against the enemies of the faith, to preserve the unity of the faith, and to defend our lords, the sick and the poor."* From this fortress 2,000 knights withheld enemy advancement into Europe several times through the centuries with many times their number. The Knights were a tremendous example of watching, standing their ground while God arose and their enemies were scattered.

3. Herrnhut, Germany, 1727 – The Great Moravian Revival

In the early 1700's, in the tiny village of Herrnhut, Germany, a remarkable move of God was born. In this village, torn apart by denominational differences, the Spirit of the Lord fell and launched a prayer movement that literally changed the course of Christian history. The strife came to a nadir in the spring of 1727. It was then that the earl of Herrnhut, Count Nikolaus Ludwig von Zinzendorf, encouraged the townsfolk to meet together to pray and worship. As they worshipped and prayed together, God's presence descended. His Spirit and their hunger inspired them to start praying unceasingly 24 hours a day 7 days a week. As they cooperated with His Spirit, God moved, the churches united, and prayer mobilized for over a hundred years. The world would never be the same again as countless revivals were sparked in Europe and America through their influence and prayers.

4. Swansea, Wales, Welsh Bible College, 1930

Rees Howells, founder of the Welsh Bible College, received a burden to intercede for nations and mobilized 24-hour prayer at the Bible College. As World War II broke out, this hidden prayer group interceded for Great Britain and allied forces. Specific strategies were prayed that became reality as seas calmed and air raids were averted leading to allied victory. Leaders of that day including Winston Churchill acknowledged God's divine intervention in protecting Great Britain through this hidden prayer group.

Become a Member of a Community Prayer Watch Group

The Azusa Street Revival began with people meeting in a house to pray. The Welsh Revival began with people meeting in a house to pray. How much more will this generation be judged – the Age of New Media – when we don't have to leave our homes? We can get on phones, log into the internet and use social media to join others in prayer and intercede for nations, for communities, for the church, for the establishment of the Kingdom, for the move of God and we can be very effective if we will dedicate one hour a day to pray.

Beloved, as you just read, groups of people joined in prayer can produce tremendous results to change the course of nations.

The amazing thing about this Pentecostal movement that gripped the world in 1906 and didn't seem to settle down until around 1915 – is that there was a prophecy given by the two fathers of the revival. The prophecy was given while the two men were at odds with one another and from two different places almost simultaneously. It is recorded that Seymour and Parham both prophesied in late 1909, on the same day – Seymour from Los Angeles and Parham in Houston – they both prophesied the Azusa glory, the shekinah glory, would return to earth after 100 years from the end of the Revival – not just in Azusa, but now it would be everywhere. Even more amazing is one of the founders of the Welsh Revival; Smith Wigglesworth confirmed the prophecy at the end of his life in 1939. It is recorded that in 1939 Smith Wigglesworth prophesied to Lester Sumrall about the final wave of God's glory. Lester Sumrall recorded that Smith Wigglesworth said:

"After that, after the third wave," he started sobbing. "I see the last day revival that's going to usher in the precious fruit of the earth. It will be the greatest revival this world has ever seen! It's going to be a wave of the gifts of the Spirit. The ministry gifts will be flowing on this

planet earth. I see hospitals being emptied out, and they will bring the sick to churches where they allow the Holy Ghost to move." – Smith Wigglesworth on Latter Rain Revival

Establishing Prayer Watches in Your Community: Join the Global Prayer Watch

If we will join others and lift up travailing prayers for God to come to town, we can war with the prophecy of these great revivalists to see the end-time revival that will sweep the globe with the charismatic gifts of the Spirit and the Lord will be present to heal. Let us never grow weary as we seek the Lord for this word to be fulfilled in our lifetime!

Truly, we cannot afford to grow weary because the battle confronting us is not about politics, gender, economics, or race—black or white, rich or poor, or one tribe or the other. But, it's a battle between life and death, light and darkness and good and evil. And, until we develop the commitment to a consistent prayer life, we cannot withstand the onslaught of hell.

Remember, in Psalm 55:17, David said, "Evening, and morning, and at noon, will I pray, and cry aloud: and he shall hear my voice," which reflects a commitment to pray at strategic times of the day and night. Like David, Daniel also prayed three times a day despite persecution, wicked plots and an evil decree against prayer (Daniel 6:10). Daniel remained faithful to his watch.

But, we have not followed in his footsteps. Compared to other religions, we are the only religion whose followers do not have a consistent prayer life. Therefore, on this note, I am calling you to join a movement of 1 million intercessors. These are men and women that I am personally charging to commit to a consistent prayer life through the deep watches of the day and night (6am to 9am, 9am to 12pm, 12pm to 3pm, 3pm to 6pm, 6pm to 9pm, 9pm to 12am, 12am to 3am, and 3am to 6am).

I have set watchmen upon thy walls, O Jerusalem, which shall never hold their peace day nor night: ye that make mention of the Lord, *keep not silence, And give him no rest, till he establish, and till he make Jerusalem a praise in the earth. (Isaiah 62:6-7, KJV)*

God is looking for watchmen—housewives, husbands, business men and women, clergy and laymen and youth alike who will stand in the gap for His agenda for families, communities and nations. He wants those who will sacrifice sleep, food and convenience to see a move of God manifest in the earth for the deliverance of our sons, daughters, husbands, wives, marketplace influencers and church leaders. After reading this book, I believe you are the one He's looking for!

Join my Global Prayer Watch for 1 or more of the 8 watches of the day and night to deploy the hand of God from heaven to affect change on the earth. Simply return the form at the back of this book or visit our website for more information.

Reasons to Be a Member of a Prayer Watch Group

1. *Create a Regular Meeting Place With God*
   a. 1 Samuel 4:16; Psalms 63:3-7; Psalms 119: 147-152; Psalms 130:5-6; Isaiah 52:8; Luke 12:37; Proverbs 8:34; Song of Solomon 3:3-4

2. *Release God's Protection for Your Nation*
   a. Nehemiah 4:7-9; Isaiah 21:6-10; Ezekiel 33:1-6

3. *Prayer Watches Are A Spiritual Warfare to Defeat the Enemy*
   a. Jeremiah 51:12; Lamentations 2:19; Daniel 7:21-22; Jeremiah 6:17

4. *Release the Strategy of the Night Watches*
   a. Genesis 32:24-29; Exodus 14:24; Judges 7:19-24; 1 Samuel 11:11; Matthew 14:24-25

5. *Establish the Kingdom of God*
   a. Psalms 127:1; Jeremiah 7:2; Daniel 4:17; Acts 9:10-18; 2 Kings 11:6; Isaiah 62:6-7

6. *Have Advanced Knowledge for Your Nation*
   a. Habakkuk 1:5; Mark 13:32-37; Revelation 16:15

7. *Pray for Revival and the Godly Prophecies of the Nation to be Fulfilled*
   a. Isaiah 62:1

8. *Promote unity and networking between churches in the community*
   a. Matthew 22:37-40

9. *Release Prayer Strategies for the Nation, Community and Leadership*
   a. Ezekiel 4:1-2

10. *Raise Spiritual Stamina of the*
   Community
   a. James 5:16

Principles To Follow In Developing A Regional
Prayer Watch

Commit to a block of time each week to pray for the region and apply the following rules for corporate prayer:

1. Come ready and willing to participate by laying aside personal concerns and agendas.
2. Release grace to all involved in the corporate prayer watch.
3. Expect God to move.
4. Always start a corporate watch by praying a blessing
5. This is easily done by participants praying a blessing for one another.
6. Personal ministry can occur during this time.
7. Imparting a blessing is an important act of worship where people come under the canopy of the Kingdom of God.
8. Use testimony time to encourage faith and sharing of answered prayers

9. Persevere in keeping an atmosphere of grace and thanksgiving in the corporate setting so that warfare can be effectual and a critical spirit is kept from developing.

10. Keep the corporate watch focused on the Lord through worship and intercession.

11. Be sure to stay with what the Holy Spirit is saying. Do not venture into areas where there is not corporate agreement.

12. Use Scriptures in prayer.

13. Keep strategies simple so that prayer can be sustained for the long haul.

14. Small groups can gain much advance by praying the 4th watch (3am-6am). For example, seven people can cover an entire week if each person took a different night each week to pray.

15. Commit to corporate gatherings on a consistent basis so that sustained Kingdom advance can be made in the spiritual climate over your region. We recommend weekly gatherings.

16. Encourage periodic corporate "soaking" times of extended worship and intercession, i.e. 12, 24, 48 hours.

17. Remember your ultimate goal is to persevere in prayer for fulfillment of prophecy and the release of Revival.

Yes! Sign me Up for a Prayer Watch! I will stand in the gap!

Please detach and complete the form fully and print legibly. This information will be used only by Prayer Summit International and will not be disclosed to other parties.

Name			
Address			
City		State	
Zip		Cell/Phone	
Email		Country	
I am committing to the following Watch:	☐1st Watch of the Day (6am to 9am) ☐2nd Watch of the Day (9am to 12pm) ☐3rd Watch of the Day (12pm to 3pm) ☐4th Watch of the Day (3pm to 6pm)	☐1st Watch of the Night (6pm to 9pm) ☐2nd Watch of the Night (9pm to 12am) ☐3rd Watch of the Night (12am to 3am) ☐4th Watch of the Night (3am to 6am)	

Return to Prayer Summit International
10320 Little Patuxent Parkway, Suite 200, Columbia, MD 21044
or scan and email to orders@prayersummitinternatinal.org
or visit
www.prayersummitinternatinal.org and look for the Join a
Prayer Watch menu item.

More Classics by the Archbishop

Binding the Strong Man

Destined to Make an Impact

Divine Timing

Enforcing Prophetic Decrees Vol. 1

Prayer Moves God

Praying Through the Promises of God

The Father Factor

The Incredible Power of a Praying Woman

The Price of Greatness

The Supernatural Power of a Praying Man

Turning Pain to Power

When Mothers Pray

All available at Amazon.com

For more information on

Archbishop Nicholas Duncan-Williams

please visit us online or contact

the office closest to you.

AFRI CA

www.actionchapel.net

www.actionchapel.tv: live streaming

+233.54.375.6884: Bookstore

+233.307.011.851: Church Office

EUROPE

www.actionchapel.org.uk

Tel: + 44.0208.952.0626

NORTH AMERICA

www.prayersummitinternational.org

+001.443.545.3808

CPSIA information can be obtained
at www.ICGtesting.com
Printed in the USA
LVHW03s1325191018
594141LV00002B/11/P